HELLO, SCAMMER

MESSING WITH THE PEOPLE WHO MESS WITH US

GEOFF KOCH

Nightengale Press

HELLO, SCAMMER
©2022 Geoff Koch

No part of this book may be reproduced or transmitted in any form or by any means, electronic or mechanical, including photocopying, recording, or by any information storage and retrieval system without written permission from the publisher, except for the inclusion of brief quotations in articles and reviews.

If you purchased this book without a cover, you should be aware that this book is stolen property. It was reported as "unsold and destroyed" to the publisher, and neither the author nor the publisher has received any payment for this "stripped book."

Library of Congress Cataloging-in-Publication Data
Koch, Geoff,
HELLO, SCAMMER! / GEOFF KOCH
ISBN 13: 978-1-945257-35-3
Genre: Humor, Non-Fiction

Published in 'the United States of America'
by Nightengale Press

December 2022
10 9 8 7 6 5 4 3 2

☙❧

Dedicated to the memory of my mother, Maridith Ann (A.D. 1942-2022), who surely would have been proud of this book—even though perhaps she'd have been slightly embarrassed by some parts of it.

☙❧

TABLE OF SCAMMERS

Credits 9
Scammerduction 10

THE CALLS

Shorts
    R2D2 22
    I'm 5 23
    Student Loan 24
    Roger 25
    How Am I Doing Today? 25
    Cancer 26

Survey calls
    Call Compensation 27
    How to Take a Phone Survey 28
    12 Wives 29

Cruise Calls
    Complimentary Cruise 31
    Poppin' a Wheelie on the Captain Cruise 32

The Patricia Series
    Which Patricia A? 38
    Melissa Kohls 41
    Homie 43
    Too Loud 43
    It's Pat 45
    I'm Sorry I Didn't Get That 47
    Sexy Voice 49
    Deeeeeep Relaxation With Alfred 50
    Migrating Monarchs 51
    How to Scare Off a Telemarketer 53

The Andrea Bell Series
- Bocce Translator 54
- Telemarketer Purgatory Line 55

Property Buyers
- Grandma! 58
- Very Superstitious (also SIMON SAYS) 60
- Booger Ghouls 62
- Reverse Survey 64

Playing Phone Jeopardy!
- Contestant Manny 71
- Contestant Dan 72

"Charity" Calls
- Verstehen Better 75
- Rip Van Ax, Exh, or Ehxs? 76
- Donation Uncertainty 80

Medical Products
- Telemarketer Reunion 83
- Telemarketer Meets the Mumbler 86

Credit Card Calls
- Should I Press "1"? 88
- Better Card Rate 90
- Yeah! 92
- Mutual Friends 95
- Hang On For Cooking 100
- π CARD 105
- XXX Telemarketer 108
- Swedish Chef 112
- Spebsnokskig The Cat (And My Birthday) 113
- Perfectly Balanced 117

Windows Tech Support Scam
- Windows Support 118
- Recruiting a Scammer to Work for Me 119

Robo-Voice Meets Multi-Voice 124
Canine Insurance 127

Brian Matthews Series
- Telepathy 128
- Telemarketer Negotiation Time! 129
- Debt Collector Confusion 133
- Brian the Dog 139
- Gettin' Testy With the Telemarketer 142

The Musical calls
- Let's Sing! 148
- Muncha Buncha Cruncha Hotline 150

Medicare Calls
- Medicare Scammers 152
- Tessi's Not Testy 157

"Simon Says" calls
- Pumpkinhead Larry 162

Internet Colors 166

"Extend Your Car's Warranty" Calls
- Model T 170
- Chili Cheese Dogs (With Fritos) 172

"Sexy Man" Calls
- Very Sexy Phone Line [also a "Simon Says" call] .. 173
- Let Me Hear Your Sexy Voice 178

Communication Problem 181

Hello, Scammer 182

THE EMAILS

Financial Scams
    Italian Heiress Maria 188
    3M 195
    Powerball Winner, Lerynne!! 198

The Good Sport 200

International Dating Scammers
    Sweetums 203
    Anastasiya the Russian Dating Scammer 205
    Nura / Knock-Knock! 231
    Linara writes Чуйка на мошенников 233
    Alesya the Aggressive Scammer 238
    Lyudmylka (and her man, Regurgitator) 248
    Elena needs Plastic Surgery 272
    Elena 2 vs. Elena 279

THE SNAIL MAILS

Song Sharks
    Sunrise Records 287

    Hilltop Records
    "Hit Haikus!" submission 293
    "Very Much Fart" submission 298
    "Free to Pee" submission 304
    "Christmas - Curious Cozy" submission 311
    The Last Laugh 314

CREDITS & ACKNOWLEDGMENTS

Editing, Layout & Design & Publication by Valerie Connelly, CEO of Nightengale Press, a Division of Nightengale Entertainment LLC

Illustrations and Cover Art by Clayton Chambers

Models: Abby Guss (as Elena)
                Victoria Borodinova (as Anastasyia)
                and numerous others from Pixabay Photos

Cover Photos: Nora Canfield

Russian Translations: Yuliya Fowler

Thank you to www.pissedconsumer.com for permission to use reports of scams posted to their website.

Web Design: Jim Stelluto

Counsel: Robert J. Notestine III

SCAMMERDUCTION

The phone rings from an unknown caller—"Scam likely".
Text message notifications ding from undetermined sources.
Emails flood your inbox promising everything
from great deals to wealth to love.
Telemarketers pester you over and again.
Aggressive, bottom-feeding debt collectors persist.
Even snail mail scams can find your mailbox.

These are the unfortunate downsides of contemporary communication. At best, the people behind it are an annoyance. At worst, they could swindle you out of a significant part your savings. These people are dedicated to concocting a variety of schemes to target you and your wallet. Sometimes their ploys are simple and straightforward; sometimes they are elaborate. Sometimes their tactics are benign, while other times they are aggressive and intimidating. When the phone rings from an unknown number, there is a good chance the call is originating from an automated phone bank half a world away using a spoofed phone number made to appear local, helmed by a foreigner who provides a fake American-sounding name. Hanging up on them doesn't stop them from calling back. If you request them to remove your name from their list, they ignore it. Like mosquitoes orbiting you on a summer's eve, they refuse to buzz off.

But what if there were ways to make these scammers eager to go away? What if they consistently hung up on you? What if every interaction ended with **them** disconnecting the call or ceasing communication? And what if you could do it with panache, frustrating them beyond their boiling point while you luxuriate in every moment of it? THAT is what this book is about. It was born out of circumstances you are surely familiar with.

HELLO, SCAMMER

The phone rings. It's someone trying to sell you something, offer some service or "you won!" You politely say no. They call back again. You tell them no again. They call back again. You tell them to remove your number. They ignore it and call back again. And again. And again. Day after day, week after week. It doesn't matter how many times you tell them to stop, they keep calling. This was my experience, and has likely been yours, as well. I soon learned that being polite was pointless. I was fed up with it.

So, I started messing with them.

Rather than hanging up or responding with genteel declinations, I began having fun with them at their expense, conceiving a new game: try to keep them on the phone as long as possible and make <u>them</u> hang up on me. I quickly discovered that people messing with them is, like a crucifix to a vampire, what they hate most. Soon, <u>all</u> of them were hanging up on me, often preceded by a flurry of profanity before slamming down the receiver.

I was on to something.

My wife at the time overheard many of these conversations and would end up laughing hysterically in the background. "You should post these on Facebook," she said. So I did. At first I posted only text transcriptions of the calls, but then later I uploaded the actual recordings. The response was (almost) universally positive –

"Do more!"

"YouTube this. You'll get a million views."

"Keep up the good work!"

"Please post more of these!"

"I've listened to this twice and just cry laughing every time! You're a genius!"

"You're my hero!"

So, I did more. Lots more. And thus messing with telemarketers and scammers became a mild habit.

I write "(almost)" universally positive because among the

responses to my pummeling of scammers was some sympathy for them. The most common objections were along the lines of: "Don't be mean to these people. **They're just doing their jobs**!" It's true that some of the tactics employed in this book could be considered "mean." However, they're also well deserved. I am not sympathetic to the claim that scammers are "just doing their jobs." And neither should you be. No one makes them be scammers. They can quit like anyone else can quit. And I know this from personal experience having once worked as a telemarketer myself—one of the very people I would have messed with.

Shortly out of collage I took an assignment through a temp agency as telemarketer at a "financial services" company. Unknown to the temp agency, I was expressly instructed to lie to the people we called. Lying was official company policy and endorsed personally by the company Boss Man. How they persisted in this without employees mutinying quickly became apparent—telescamming operations have a bizarre office environment.

In this one, every morning 60-ish moderately graying Boss Man would assemble his full roster of (mostly) young employees in his sprawling personal office to hold court, crowding in some couple dozen full-time and temporary staff combined. He would spend a good ten to fifteen minutes lecturing everyone from the most recent corporate motivational pablum cassette, book or seminar he'd just absorbed. The office was adorned with trite, framed corporate motivational posters littering its walls such as:

HELLO, SCAMMER

COMMITMENT
Energy, Power and Will.
The required, potent mix to reach Success.

EXCELLENCE
To excel is a determined choice,
not a pre-determined destiny.

Yack. I once displayed my own self-made motivational poster that read: "I'm pink, therefore I'm spam" emblazoned over Rodin's "The Thinker." They didn't like it. But I digress. In the midst of these "artistic" wall adornments, Boss Man would randomly call on an employee to put on the spot for a pop quiz based one of his previous day's lectures:

"Sandra! What are the 10 principles of effective management?"

As if being jolted with electricity, poor Sandra bolted upright in her chair, then closed her eyes with an intense focus as if her very existence depended on it. She started reciting.

"Okay. *sigh* Principle number one is… (blah blah blah). Number two is (blah blah…)"

After completing her deca-recitation, Boss Man dramatically paused, scanned the room, then pronounced judgment up her performance:

HELLO, SCAMMER

"Very good."

Sandra relaxed.

"Did everyone hear that?" he probed, keenly examining the assembled company. Everyone nodded wide-eyed. The entire company walked on eggshells around this guy. He would then drone on with more corporate motivational word salad. Finally, in a hushed but vehement tone he dismissed us with:

"Now… Go!"

His arm shot up pointing everyone out of his office door. We were unleashed for the day upon the rest of the unsuspecting world.

On day one, they placed a script in front of me (and all the other telescammers) that Boss Man declared was "scientifically designed." We were to recite this script to our victims *verbatim* to induce them to engage the companies $ervice$. We were **not** to deviate from it one iota! We were also given thick stacks of names and numbers of our "targets" to call—none of which requested to be on the list, of course. Then we began calling. Once the target answered, I started reading the script. Given that the script felt stilted to my speaking style, I modified it throughout the day by scratching out various words and phrases, replacing them with how I would more naturally say it. It seemed to improve my results. But this did not go over well with Boss Man.

On day two of this telescamming job I walked into my miserable little half-cubicle to discover my modified script was gone. "Strange," I thought, "but no big deal. I'll just grab another 'scientifically designed' script from the official box where they were kept,"—Yes, there was actually a prominently displayed "official script box" centrally located in the office—"and modify it again as best I can remember." So I did.

About thirty minutes into the day, in the midst of a call, Boss Man marched into my half-cubicle and furiously snatched my newly modified script off my desk, slamming down another fresh, untainted one in its place. He screamed while lording over me, "You WILL NOT deviate from the script! These are 'scientifically designed!' DO YOU UNDERSTAND?!?"

Oh my. What did I get myself into here? To compound the misery of this mini-tyrant's reign, he had specifically instructed us to lie as part of the job.

An employee question was posed at that morning's company pow-wow regarding unavailable targets: "What do we say to them if the person is not available?" Boss Man smugly answered that we were to "Leave a message and tell the message taker that this was a *personal* call' to induce them to call back," he said with a sly smile. He knew what he was asking us to do and was quite pleased with himself for it. It obviously was not a personal call. So when the target called back, we would simply ignore the caller's "personal call" expectations and start reciting the "scientifically designed" script and commercial $$ solicitations. Most targets would politely listen, but one—and I'll never forget this—interrupted me mid-spiel and very irritatedly objected:

"Wait a minute! I was told this was a *personal* call. That's not true. THIS IS NOT A PERSONAL CALL."

I was instantly deflated, caught in "my" lie. After pausing for a moment to collect my thoughts, I sighed and acknowledged his assessment.

"You're absolutely right. It's not a personal call. We just say that in the message to get you to call back."

He thanked me for my honesty and hung up. This was midway through day two of the job.

I quit right then.

Another telemarketing job I did was more benign. This job was to raise money for a well-known established and legitimate charity. We didn't solicit money directly from those we called, but rather got them to recruit people to raise the money themselves in a fun and creative way. It was a very clever money-raising tactic. But we were still calling people unsolicited which resulted in a many people becoming understandably irritated, often gifting me with an earful of profanity before screaming, "Take me off your list!!" And I did take their number off of *my* list—though that didn't necessarily mean they were taken off of the *company's* list. Sneaky. But most people I spoke with were polite and willing to hear what I had to say—which eventually clued me into why so many targets could be turned into victims if the caller had nefarious intentions.

As I continued with my charitable telemarketing job for the next several weeks I happened upon a phenomenon. When I started the job my "Yes" responses were only about 20% of all calls I made. This was rather discouraging, especially compared to other telemarketers who had much better "Yes" rates. However, through experimentation I discovered that by changing the tone and cadence of my voice, as well as by changing the language of the script to suit by speaking style—we were allowed to modify the call script in this job, versus the, ahem, previous one—I could dramatically up my "Yes" response rate. So, as I relaxed my telepitch delivery and tone, my response rate went from around 80% *"No's"* to 80% *"Yes's."* Incredible. And I was selling the exact same thing. Delivery and interaction style were the only things that changed. In short, I learned that people could be *easily manipulated*.

In the case of the charity telemarketing job, it could be argued that the manipulation was harmless, even beneficial. However, in the hands of people with ill intent, this can cause tremendous damage. The lesson: the people on the other end of the interaction may be highly skilled at manipulating you in order to exploit your goodwill. Indeed, you'll see in many of the calls that follow, once their mask is off and veneer scratched, the people revealed underneath are quite heinous.

So, all that to say—*please* do not feel bad for these people. No

HELLO, SCAMMER

one makes them do these jobs. They should be like me, quit and find another job—something respectable, productive and actually beneficial to society. There is no excuse for harassing and scamming others. So, feel free to use the interactions in this book as templates for your own interactions with scammers, 100% conscience-free! Have fun with it. Scammers will only stop trying to scam others when they realize not only have their efforts been in vain, but also their intended victim relished every moment of having turned the tables on them. Enjoy it. And spread the word that we're onto you, scammers, and absolutely loving wasting your time.

So, grab some popcorn and let's dive in. As you'll see, I do not hang up on them, **they hang up on me**. *Every* phone interaction ends with the scammer HANGING UP or GOING AWAY. By the time you've completed this book, you should have copious amounts of inspiration to deal with these people with aplomb. So now, it's time to say—

Hello, Scammer.

The events in this book are all real communications with unknown callers that were initiated by them, not the Author. In some cases these callers may claim to be affiliated with companies or products not solicited by the Author, or whose affiliation is unknown and not verified by the companies and could not be verified by the Author. These unknown callers may be misusing those company names or products without that company's consent. The Author and Publisher assume no liability based upon the representations made in communications by these callers. These communications are merely being relayed to you, dear reader, "as is" as they actually happened with no opinion about the companies or products themselves.

THE CALLS

Visit **helloscammer.com** to order the accompanying double-CD set of all the recordings in this book.

Own your copy forever!

Scan to order:

How do you know it's a scammer?

It's quite simple. The Author presumes all unsolicited calls and communications from unknown people to be scams until proven otherwise. This is a healthy presumption for your wallet, and has generally been proven to be true. Err on the side of caution and don't let unknown callers take advantage of your good will.

THE CALLS

All calls in this book are real. None are scripted, planned, or involve friends or actors. Scammers initiated all calls in this book—they called me. The goal for every call is to keep them on the phone as long as possible, which averages to 2-3 minutes before they hang up in amusement, frustration or rage. Some scammers hang on for several minutes longer – the current record is 13 minutes. What troopers. They deserve a lollipop. The goal for each call varies. Sometimes it's to get them to say ridiculous things[1], sometimes it's to confound, or sometimes it's to spar; though it's always to waste as much of their time as possible AND to entertain *us*. This part of *Hello, Scammer* consists of authentic call transcripts. The offenders' full names and other personal information have been redacted to protect the guilty. Most calls have the actual recordings you can listen to in the included audio, all of which are real. None are planned or staged. Play the corresponding track on the CD[2]/audio links/QR code and revel in aural bliss. As mentioned, you will notice a consistent pattern with these calls – they all end with the scammer/telemarketer hanging up, often furiously. Good. When you emulate these methods, bets are you will hear them hanging up on you, too. Every time. And like me, you may relish it to the core of your bosom.

Now let's mess with them, shall we?

---

1 e.g. See "Very Superstitious"
2 Get your own CD at helloscammer.com. Own your copy forever!

Shorts

R2D2

TeleMarketer: How are you today?

Me: I am so good I couldn't be any better even if I tried!

TM: Well, that's great. Now this call may be monitored and recorded for quality and training purposes, okay?

Me: I was just about to tell you the same thing!

TM: Not a problem, sir. Also let me give you my corporate ID number.

LISTEN
CD 1, TRACK 1

Me: Okay.

TM: Now that is B as in boy.

Me: Uh huh.

TM: Q as in queen.

Me: Yup.

TM: 1094.

Me: Thanks for that. Hey, do you want my number also?

TM: And… and um, sure.

Me: Okay. It's R, and then 2 like the number "2." And then D, like the letter "D." And then number "2" again. Got it?

TM: Okay. And this identifies you as…?

Me: R2D2.

TeleMarketer:

22

I'M 5

This telemarketer thought he was talking to a 5-year-old.

TELEMARKETER:
Thank you for calling, this is Dennis. How can I help you?

Me: (emulating a child's voice): Who?

TM: Dennis. We are _____ tax relief.

Me: (child's voice): I'm 5!
5 years old.

TM: (confused pause) Hello?

Me: Hello!

TM: Hello, hello!

Me: Hi! I'm 5!

TM: (changes to more delicate tone of voice as if speaking to a child): Yeah, hi there! This call is in regards to a tax-related matter. Um. Are you or somebody in need of tax services?

Me: Wanna hear me burp?

TM: Excuse me?

Me: *** BELCH ***
Wanna hear me burp again?

TELEMARKETER:

HELLO, SCAMMER

Shorts

STUDENT LOAN

An automated robocaller lovingly rings to offer debt relief for student loans. Of course, I press 1 to take advantage of this exciting offer.

LISTEN
CD 1, TRACK 3

TeleMarketer:
    National student loan help center, may I have your name please?
Me: I am sooo happy to hear from you guys!
TM: You have a student loan, sir?
Me: Oh yeah! I love those things. I got some.
TM: Is it for federal loans?
Me: Yeah, I got like 12 of them.

TeleMarketer:

HELLO, SCAMMER

Shorts

ROGER?

TeleMarketer:
   Can I speak to Roger?

Me: Who?

TM: Can I just speak with the man or the woman of the house?

Me: Which would you like me to be?

TeleMarketer:

HOW AM I DOING TODAY?

TeleMarketer:
   How are you doing today?

Me: A tiny bit achy. Feeling a little thirsty at the moment. Definitely hungry. Feel I need to stretch then exercise. Then feeling antsy to get some work done. I also feel today like...

TeleMarketer:

Shorts

HELLO, SCAMMER

CANCER

Me: Hello?

TeleMarketerRobot:

("bloop") Hi! My name is Lisa. I'm calling from _____. This is just a quick survey call. Has someone in your household been diagnosed with cancer, leukemia, or any type of lymphoma?

LISTEN
CD 1, TRACK 4

Me: Yeah. Yeah, unfortunately. Yup.

TMR: Please stay on the line while I transfer your call to my supervisor.

(pause)

LiveTeleScammer:

Thank you for staying online. You were having a word with one of my associates. I believe somebody may have been diagnosed with cancer in the past, is that true?

Me: Yeah, I'm a cancer.

LTS: Ok, what kind of cancer do you have?

Me: It's the **zodiac sign** kind.

LTS: (silence)

Me: Hello?

LiveTeleScammer:

HELLO, SCAMMER

Survey Calls

CALL COMPENSATION

TeleMarketer:
- May I speak with _____?

Me: Wait, who are you?

TM: My name is Mary and I'm with _____ Research. Can I ask you a few questions?

Me: Sure, but let me ask you one first. Are you doing this for free?

TM: Oh yes, this survey is totally free!

Me: No, I mean are you working for free today making these calls?

TM: [pause] Uh, no.

Me: Ok, so you're getting paid, right?

TM: [pause] Yes.

Me: And so the company you're working for is also getting paid, right?

TM: Uh... yes.

Me: Great. So the information you're gathering from me is valuable to someone, isn't it?

TM: Um.... Could you just answer a few questions, sir?

Me: Sure I could! But since my answers are **valuable**, you need to **cut me in on the deal**. I get paid, too.

TM: Uh... This will just take a few minutes, sir.

Me: I'm glad to hear that. But I'll need to be PAID UPFRONT for my answers. When can I get my payment?

[long pause]

TM: You have a nice day, sir.

Me: Aw. Will you call back?

TeleMarketer:
- No.

HELLO, SCAMMER

Survey Calls

HOW TO TAKE A PHONE SURVEY

TeleMarketer: Hi! Would you be willing to take a brief survey regarding your recent experience with (Company)?

Me: Sure.

TM: Ok! How would you rate your recent experience with (Company)?

Me: Pretty good.

TM: ...Hold on. Would you say: Very satisfied, somewhat satisfied, or not satisfied at all?

Me: Pretty good.

TM: Um, that's not one of the choices. Would you say: Very satisfied, somewhat satisfied, or not satisfied at all?

Me: I just told you "pretty good." Twice.

TM: Well that's not one of the choices.

Me: So? You called me. That's my choice.

TM: Okay, moving on. How likely are you to recommend (Company) to your friends or family..?

Me: I might recommend it under the right circumstances.

TM: ...Hold on. Would you say: Highly likely, somewhat likely, or not likely at all?

Me: As I said, I might recommend it.

TM: Sir, that's not one of the choices.

Me: And that's my problem because... why?

TM: Sir, do you not want to take the survey?

Me: I have been taking the survey.

TM: Sir, you have to pick one of the answers.

HELLO, SCAMMER

Survey Calls

Me: Says who?

TeleMarketer:

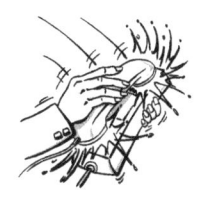

12 WIVES

TeleMarketer:
Hi, my name is Victor with Survey _____ on a recorded line. How are you doing today?

Me: I'm doing just, ya know, pretty darn good!

TM: Well that's good to hear. Now, you may be entitled to financial compensation. It was indicated during our survey that yourself or a loved one had suffered side effects from an IVC filter implant. Was this correct?

Me: Hmmmm. Let me think about that for a minute... Um, let's see... It might have been one of my wives. Um, hmm. Which one are you talking about?

TM: (pause)... Well, I'm asking you, sir. Like, do you know of any loved ones or family members who had an IVC filter implant?

Me: Well, I'm still thinking because I got a REALLY big family. Cuz I've got like **12 wives**. So I'm trying to think of which one it might have been. Can you help me with that?

TM: (pause)... Sir, unfortunately I'd be unable to assist you with that.

Me: Huh. That's too bad. We're gonna have to talk through this then, try to figure out which one it might have been. Let's see... What was the problem again?

LISTEN

CD 1, TRACK 5

HELLO, SCAMMER

Survey Calls

TM: There's no problem. Sir, I do thank you for your time and I hope you have a great day, okay?

An Automated Telemarketer Voice takes over....

ATV: Thank you for completing the survey! Your entry is now complete. Goodbye!

HELLO, SCAMMER

Cruise Calls

COMPLIMENTARY CRUISE

Prior to this call an automated system called to survey my "eligibility" for a free cruise. Of course I answered yes to all the Bot's questions, then this live human called me...

TeleMarketer:
Hello, you have received a complimentary Bahamas cruise!

Me: Wow, that's freaking AWESOME!

TM: Yes! I just need to ask you a few questions. Did you answer a phone survey this morning?

Me: Hmmm... Which one? I've already taken around 30 surveys just this morning.

TM: 30?

Me: Maybe it was more like 50.

TM: What are you, some sort of surveyor?

Me: More like a survey-ee!

TM: "Survey-ee"? Uh... well if I could just get your name.

Me: I have different names for different surveys. Which survey?

TM: Look, I don't care. Just give me a name... Mr. Smith, Mr. Jones...

Me: How about Brian.

TM: Okay, Brian. So Brian, what we do is give people unused cabins on cruise ships... BLAH BLAH BLAH.... I just need to ask you three qualifying questions. Brian, are you over 18, are you available to travel within the next 18 months, and do you have valid credit card?

Me: Well, all I want to know is — can I water ski behind the cruise ship?

TeleMarketer:
Sir, please disregard this call.

HELLO, SCAMMER

Cruise Calls

POPPIN' A WHEELIE ON THE CAPTAIN CRUISE

I got tag teamed by a couple scamming telemarketers who called to offer a "free" Bahamas cruise...

LISTEN
CD 1, TRACK 6

TELEMARKETER KAYLA:
　　Hi, my name is Kayla. I'm a senior travel coordinator in the promotions department. I'm here to help you claim your complimentary cruise for two.

Me:　Aww yeah!

TMK:　This call may be monitored or recorded for quality and training purposes.

Me:　I love that.

TMK:　Who do I have the pleasure of speaking with?

Me:　Awwwww yeah! Yeah, yeah, yeah, yeah, yeah, yeah, YEAH! Hey! Bwian!

TMK:　Bwian?

Me:　Yeah, Bwian.

TMK:　B-W-A-Y-N

Me:　Yeah, close enough.
　　(Hearing lots of noise and people talking in the background).
　　So wait, are you guys partying on the cruise ship already?! You guys got a party going on back there?

TMK:　I'm sorry, was that how you spelt [sic] it?

Me:　Yeah yeah, close enough. So you guys partying on the cruise ship already?

HELLO, SCAMMER

Cruise Calls

TMK: No sir, we're in the promotions department. We're in a building.

Me: You don't got a party?

TMK: No. No party going on.

Me: But Kayla, it's Friday.

TMK: Um, it is Friday.

Me: Well, at least you're knocking back a few, right?

TMK: I'm sorry. What?

Me: You guys should be just like knocking back a few brewskies. Ya know what I mean?
(stupid falsetto:) Woot woot woot!
Friday! Ya know what I'm sayin, some brewskies? Heh?

TMK: No, we don't do that in the promotions department, sir.

Me: Awwwwww. So check it out, Kayla. Remember last year you called me and you hooked me up with another free cruise?
It's Kayla, right?

TMK: Kayla, yeah.

Me: Yeah, ok. So, last year, Kayla, you called me and you hooked me up with another free cruise. And guess what? I'm on that cruise RIGHT NOW, and lemme tell you, Kayla, it's freakin' AWESOME.

TMK: Um sir, you didn't talk to me last year.

Me: Huh. You sure it wasn't you?

TMK: Nope.

Me: Well then, it was someone that sounded just like TOTALLY like you! That's totally weird.
So check it out, Kayla. So the dude in the cabin next to me also got a free cruise from you guys last year.

HELLO, SCAMMER

Cruise Calls

              And he's on that cruise right now also!

TMK: It wasn't with us then, sir.

Me: Huh. Weird. Anyway, but he got the *CAPTAIN CRUISE*. You know what that is?

TMK: No I don't, sir.

Me: You know like sometimes the captain is off? So, when the captain's off, you get to be the captain of the ship!

TMK: Yeah, but sir, you didn't get that cruise from us, then.

Me: And you know what else? That dude actually >>*popped a wheelie*<< with the cruise ship! Did you know a cruise ship can pop a wheelie, Kayla?

Kayla mutes her line for a moment, probably getting her supervisor to listen in.

Me: Hey, Kayla? Kayla?

TMK: (back on the line): I'm here.

Me: So when the captain's off, you get to be the captain of the ship! Isn't that freaking awesome?? I tell you, the whole ship was FREAKING OUT with the wheelie.
Could you hear me, Kayla?

TMK: I heard you say that you had… the captain did a wheelie.

Me: No, no. It was the dude in the cabin **next** to me that got the Captain Cruise and popped the wheelie. Lemme tell you something. Chicks dig a dude who can pop a cruise ship wheelie. You know what I'm saying? You know what I'm saying, Kayla?? Uh? UH?
(annoying falsetto:) Woot woot!

HELLO, SCAMMER

Cruise Calls

TMK: So... you're saying you got a cruise from us last year, you're on the cruise today, the guy next to you told you... right now you're on the cruise. The guy next door to you told you he got the same cruise from us, and he got the "Captain Cruise"...

Me: Yeah.

TMK: ...and being that the captain is off, he got to be the captain...

Me: Yup.

TMK: ...and he being the captain, and being that he's the captain, you got him to do a wheelie on the ship.

Me: Right. And chicks dig that dude. You know what I'm saying, Kayla?

TMK: Alright. (Kayla mutes her line again)

Me: So Kayla. You GOT to hook me up with a Captain Cruise. You know what I mean? So... can you hook me up with a Captain Cruise?

TMK: (silence)

Me: Kayla?

Kayla has enough and tags out.

Dude TeleMarketer (DTM) – probably her supervisor – then takes over as Kayla got in over her head. He tries to steamroll over me and close the deal – in vain.

DUDE TELEMARKETER:

No, absolutely! I'm really a man. But, do you have a pen and paper with you?

Me: Wait, what happened to Kayla?

DTM: Do you have a pen and paper with you?

HELLO, SCAMMER

Cruise Calls

Me: Wait, where's Kayla?

DTM: I am Kayla.

Me: Well your voice just dropped like 3 octaves.

DTM: Yeah, yeah. I was born a male.

Me: Freaky!

DTM: Do you have your pen and paper with you?

Me: Yeah. So can you hook me up with a Captain Cruise?

DTM: Yeah, you'll get the **captain's dinner** on the return passage. Best in the Bahamas.

(Note he switcherooed "Captain Cruise" to "captain's dinner." You're so sneaky, DTM.)

Me: Freakin' awesome.

DTM: Yeah. So we're gonna give you the cruise for free.

Me: Awesome.

DTM: All you pay are the port taxes, only 59 for you, 59 for the second person.

Me: Awesome.

DTM: Right.

Me: Love it.

DTM: Ok, for the port taxes, did you want to use your Visa, Mastercard or Discover?

Me: Um, let's see. Discover. But I'm gonna use my *Special* Discover Card. So, in order to process your request for my payment, I need to get your credit card number and process it. So could I get your credit card number, please?

DTM: What type of card? You said you want to use your Discover. Should start with a 6011.

Me: Yeah but this is a *Special* Discover Card.

HELLO, SCAMMER

Cruise Calls

DTM: There's no such thing as a Special Discover Card.

Me: Yeah, there is. I got one right here!

DTM: I've been dealing with cards since 2003. What do you mean?

Me: Can I just get your credit card number so I can get my cruise, please?

DTM: Sure. We'll go ahead pass on your free cruise. But I do appreciate your time, okay?

Me: Wait, wait, wait. My Captain Cruise!

TELEMARKETERS:

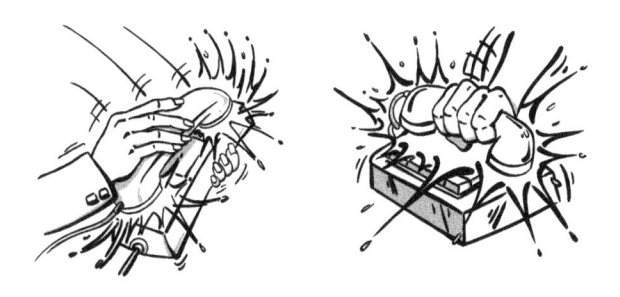

HELLO, SCAMMER

THE PATRICIA SERIES

For months I received a series of phone calls for "Patricia Nelson," most of which were from bottom-feeding bill collectors. Sounds like "Patricia" may have skipped town by giving them what she thought was a phony phone number—mine. Unfortunately for them, they got me instead. Doubly unfortunately for them, they started getting on my nerves...

THE PATRICIA SERIES #1
WHICH PATRICIA "A"?

BILL COLLECTOR:
Yes, good morning. My name is Delores _____ and this entire call will be monitored...

Me: That's great!!

BC: ... or recorded for quality assurance.

LISTEN
CD 1, TRACK 7

Me: I LOVE quality insurance.

BC: Okay, I was looking for a Patricia Nelson.

Me: Is this uh, Delores?

BC: It is.

Me: Oh, hey, Delores! Yeah. Which... You said, who are you looking for again?

BC: Patricia. Nelson.

Me: (thinking hard): Patricia... Patricia Nelson... Hang on a sec.

BC: Thank you.

Me: I'm sorry, which Patricia Nelson do you want? There's about FIVE of them here.

BC: Oooh, I just know it's Patricia **A** Nelson.

Me: Patricia **A** Nelson?

BC: Mmm-huh.

HELLO, SCAMMER
THE PATRICIA SERIES

Me: There's about FOUR Patricia **A** Nelsons here. Which one do you want?

BC: Oh my goodness. I... I don't know which one it is, sir. I don't know her personally.

Me: Oh, you don't?

BC: No, I do not.

Me: Oh. Well then um... hmmm. Then why are you calling for her then?

BC: Oh, I can't disclose the nature of the call without her permission.

Me: Well, we'll get it. Well hold on.(yelling off phone): Hey! Patricia A! Delores wants to talk to you, is that okay? (back on phone): Yeah, she said "It's cool."

BC: I'm sorry?

Me: Yeah. Patricia A said it was cool. Patricia <u>Ann</u> did.

BC: What was cool?

Me: To talk to you.

BC: No, I need her on the phone to give me permission, Sir.

Me: No, she's busy right now.

BC: I'll try her back at another time.

Me: Hold on. Did you want Patricia <u>Allison</u> maybe?

BC: I... I don't know what. All I know is the middle initial is "A." I have no idea what the name is.

Me: Well, then, I mean which one, how do I know which one to get for you?

BC: I....

Me: Because there's Patricia <u>Ann</u>. Patricia <u>Allison</u>. There's Patricia...

BC: 1963 is the year of birth.

Me: ...<u>Abby</u>. They're all born in 1963. Patricia <u>Allison</u>. Patricia <u>Abby</u>. Patricia <u>Amber</u>. And I think there's also Patricia <u>Allie</u>.

39

HELLO, SCAMMER

THE PATRICIA SERIES

BC: Okay, all right. Thank you for your time, sir. You have a good day.

Me: Well wait! Hold on. We're just getting interesting here. So what's going on?

BC: Again sir, I cannot disclose the nature of the call without her permission.

Me: I just got it to you.

BC: I beg your pardon?

Me: Well, Patricia <u>Ann</u> said it was okay. Do you want Patricia <u>Allison</u>? Do you want her permission?

BC: And again I have to tell you Sir, it just says Patricia <u>A</u> Nelson. I do not know what the middle name is. There's just an "A" up there.

Me: Then how do you know which one?

BC: I don't know which one, Sir. That's what I'm trying to tell you.

Me: Well then why are you calling here?

BC: All right Sir, I'm gonna… I'm gonna discontinue the call. You have a good day.

Me: Wait!

Bill Collector:

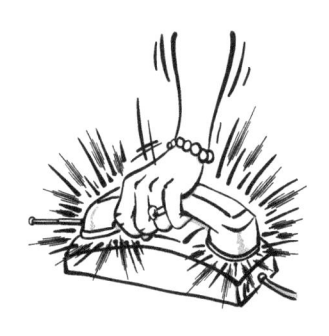

THE PATRICIA SERIES #2
MELISSA KOHLS

BILL COLLECTOR:
    I'm calling for Patricia Nelson. I'm calling from Kohls department stores.

Me: Oh, at Kohls?

BC: Yes, Sir.

Me: And what was your name?

BC: Melissa.

Me: Melissa!

BC: Yes, sir.

Me: Melissa...?

BC: From Kohls.

Me: Melissa Kohl?

BC: No, from Kohls department stores.

Me: Oh, okay. So that means not Melissa Kohl.

BC: No, sir! (laughs)

Me: Oh, okay. Is it another "K" though?

BC: I'm sorry?

Me: Is your last name with another "K"? I can guess. Is it... Kessler? Melissa <u>Kessler</u>?

BC: Ooooohhh, no Sir. That's not my last name.

Me: Oh, okay. Is it Melissa... <u>Kelley</u>?

BC: No, sir. We don't...

Me: Okay. Is it Melissa... <u>Krackle</u>?

BC: Okay, sir. Is Patricia Nelson available?

Me: Well, I need to find out what your last name is first.

BC: We don't provide our last names, sir. I can give you my last four numbers of my ID if you need that.

Me: So there's like a bunch of you on the phone?

LISTEN
CD 1, TRACK 8

HELLO, SCAMMER

THE PATRICIA SERIES

BC: We're in a whole big area. It's a big room. There's a bunch of us around here.

Me: Oh really? Like you guys having a party?

BC: I'm sorry?

Me: You guys having a party?

BC: No, sir. Again, if Miss Patricia Nelson's not available please let me know so that we can give her a call back later. If she is, I would like to speak with her, please.

Me: Well I mean, I wanna join the party. I wanna know where you guys are partying cuz we got some Jäger here.

BC: Okay, sir. I'm gonna have to guess she's not available. So then I will go ahead and give her a call back later. I appreciate the time.

Me: Is it Melissa... <u>Kraygle</u>?

BC: Okay. I'm gonna ask one more time, sir, because these calls are recorded. Is Patricia Nelson available?

Me: Is it Melisssa....

BC: Have a great day, sir.

Me: ...<u>Kankles</u>? Is it **Kankles**?

BILL COLLECTOR:

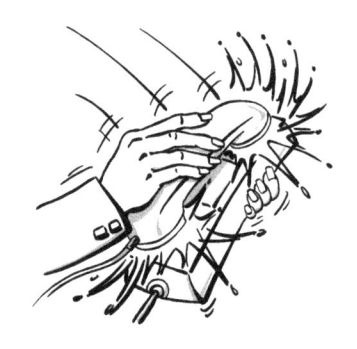

HELLO, SCAMMER

THE PATRICIA SERIES

THE PATRICIA SERIES #3
HOMIE

Me: (friendly sounding): Hello?

BILL COLLECTOR:
Yes, may I speak with Patricia Nelson?

Me: Okay.
(switching to a deep, ghetto voice): Yo, YO! Dis Patricia. WHASSUP??

BC: (silence)

Me: HELLOOOOW?

BILL COLLECTOR:

LISTEN
CD 1, TRACK 9

THE PATRICIA SERIES #4
TOO LOUD

BILL COLLECTOR:
Hi, I was trying to reach Patricia.

Me: Ow! Ow ow ow ow ow!!(just above a whisper): Sorry. I'm sorry. Your voice is really hurting my ears. Can you talk a little bit more quietly, please?

BC: (slightly quieter): Is Patricia available...?

Me: Owwww! Ow ow ow. I'm sorry. I'm on this medication...

BC: So is Patricia available?

LISTEN
CD 1, TRACK 10

43

HELLO, SCAMMER

THE PATRICIA SERIES

Me: Oww!! Ow ow. ...it makes my hearing really sensitive. Can you please talk, like just whisper?

BC: (slightly quieter still): I am whispering. Is she available..?

Me: Ow. That's still... shhhhh. I'm sorry that's still, I'm still a little sensitive.
(whispering): Can you just whisper?

BC: (much louder): Okay, you can hear what I'm saying! I'm try to reach Patricia Nelson...

Me: OWWWW! Ow, ow!!! Are you trying to hurt me?

BC: I'm trying...

Me: OWWWWW!

BC: ...to reach...

Me: OWW!!

BC: ...Patricia Nelson.

Me: Jeez! SHHHHHHH!!!

BC: This is a serious matter.

Me: (whispering): Shhhhhh! Shhh. I wanna talk to you but it's too loud.

BC: I need to speak to her...

Me: Ow!

BC: ...or representing attorney.

Me: OWW! Dangit.
(super whispering): Why do you want to torment me like this?

BC: Okay, this is not...

Me Ow.

TM ...this is not...

Me: ow

BC: This is...

Me: Ow!

BC: ...a serious matter.

44

HELLO, SCAMMER

THE PATRICIA SERIES

Me: Owww! Shhhhhh!
BC: So may I speak to Patricia?
Me: (whispering): You're gonna have to talk more quietly.
BC: Disconnecting the call.
(silence)
Me: Now it's quiet. That's better.

BILL COLLECTOR:

THE PATRICIA SERIES #5
IT'S PAT

Fooled this collector into thinking he was talking with two people, me and "Pat"...

BILL COLLECTOR:
(with a heavy middle eastern accent): This is Aaahlin, I'm calling from _____ auto finance. Is Pahhhtricia Nelsons available?

LISTEN
CD 1, TRACK 11

Me: (friendly voice): Oh, you're calling for Pat?
BC: Oooh, I'm sorry but I cannot disclose that information, sir. So I just want to ask if Pahhtricia Nelson is available?
Me: Oh yeah, just a sec!
(talking off phone as if for someone else): Hey, Pat!

HELLO, SCAMMER

THE PATRICIA SERIES

      ("someone else" super deep grumpy voice – "Pat"): Yeah??

      (friendly voice): It's for you! Phone's for you!

      (Gruff Pat voice): Meh.

      (friendly voice): Come on, take it!

      (Gruff Pat voice): **grumbling**

Shuffling in the background, then "Pat" gets on the phone…

Me: (Gruff Pat voice): Hey! This is PAT.

BC: (slightly nervous): Hello, on a recorded line. Am I speaking to Miss Pahhtricia Nelson?

"Pat": (Gruff Pat voice): Used to be. This is PAT.

BC: Um. Am I speaking Pahhtricia Nelson? Is that a yes?

"Pat": It's PAT now. I'm in transition.

BC: Mmm huh. So this is Pahtricia Nelson, right?

"Pat": No! It's PAT. It's PAT now. Used to be Patricia. Now it's PAT. I'm in transition.

BC: Oh, I see.

"Pat": Do you get it?

BC: Ah. Okay. So it's Pat Nelson..?

"Pat": Hey! Lemme tell you something. I just had my BALLS put on the other day. And I tell you what. Hey, let me tell you something. Dude. I get it now, the ball scratching thing. I GET it. You know, you're sittin' in front of the TV, and you got like, you know, Packers on and a brewsky in one hand and you just got an ITCH sometimes. And it's just like, "GrrrrrRRrrrrRrr… Yeah!" Dude, I get it now. I GET IT. You with me?

BC: Yes. Mmm-huh. So by the way, this is Aahlin. I'm calling from _____ auto finance. We just want to confirm, sir, if I'm speaking to Pat Nelson. Is that a yes?

"Pat": The other thing about this thing is, you know… I like FOOTBALL more now than I ever did before. So I GET it.

HELLO, SCAMMER

THE PATRICIA SERIES

You see, I'm gittin' it! Ever since I got my balls put on it's just, "YEAH!!"

BILL COLLECTOR:
Thank you so much for taking my call.

THE PATRICIA SERIES #6
SORRY, I DIDN'T GET THAT

Pretending to be a **malfunctioning automated phone system** has its perks. Especially when the scammer falls for it.

BILL COLLECTOR:
Hi, thanks for calling[1] _____ this is Shantoy. How may I assist you?

Me: (feigning an automated answering voice):
Hello! Thank you for calling! Who are you calling for, please?

BC: Just a moment. (pause) We're trying to reach Patricia Nelson.

Me: Patricia Nelson.
Is that correct?

BC: Yes, sir.

Me: Thank you for calling Patricia Nelson's line! To connect with Patricia Nelson, please press 1.

BC: (Presses "1")
BEEP

LISTEN
CD 1, TRACK 12

---
[1] I did not call them, they called *me*.

HELLO, SCAMMER

THE PATRICIA SERIES

Me: I'm sorry, I didn't get that. Could you please try again?

BC: (Presses "1" again)
BEEP

Me: I'm sorry, I didn't get that. Could you please try again one more time please?

BC: (Repeatedly presses "1")
BEEP BEEP BEEP BEEP BEEP BEEP BEEP

Me: I'm sorry, I didn't get that. Could you please try again?

BC: (long pause)
BEEP
Hello?

Me: It sounds like you're having trouble. Hold for one moment, please.

BC: BEEP
(pause)

Me: Thank you for calling Patricia Nelson line. To connect with Patricia Nelson, please press 1.

BC: (Presses "1") BEEP

Me: I'm sorry, I didn't get that. Could you please try again?

BILL COLLECTOR:

HELLO, SCAMMER
THE PATRICIA SERIES

THE PATRICIA SERIES #7
SEXY VOICE

Success #2 duping the scammer into thinking he's talking with two people...

BILL COLLECTOR:
    Hello. We're looking for Patricia.

Me: Who?

BC: Patricia.

Me: Patricia?

BC: Yeah.

Me: Okay. Hold.

    (pause – I now become "Patricia")

Me: (strangely emulating a high woman's voice): Hellllooo!

BC: Yeah hi, Patricia. My name is Chris with _____. How are you?

Me: (weird woman voice): HHhhhHiiii!

BC: Yup. So just calling about your property in _____ Drive because we're looking to buy two more properties. I was wondering if you'd consider selling it?

Me: You have a ssssexy voice!

BC: (SILENCE...)

Me: Hhhhhiiii?

BILL COLLECTOR:

HELLO, SCAMMER

THE PATRICIA SERIES

THE PATRICIA SERIES #8
DEEEEEEP RELAXATION WITH ALFRED

Alfred the Bill Collector called. He didn't know that he phoned someone in a deeeeep state of relaxation...

Me: I'm sorry, could you start over again please?

BILL COLLECTOR:
Okay. Hello, this is Alfred _____. The entire call will be monitored or recorded for quality assurance. May I speak to Patricia A. Nelson?

Me: (In a veeerrry relaxed, catatonic voice): Ohh. Alfred?

BC: Yes?

Me: Ohhhhh. I've been expecting your call. So nice to hear from you.

LISTEN
CD 1, TRACK 13

BC: (puzzled/bemused):
Ooo-kay. Um, is Patricia A. Nelson available though?

Me: I'm sorry, who are you with again?

BC: Monarch _____.

Me: (nearly whispering): Mooooonarrrrch. So glad to hear from you all.

Alfred, have you ever been in state of relaxation so deep that you just... *sigh* ... feel like you're floating and not a care in the world?

BC: (confused pause)
Okay, what was that again you said? I didn't catch everything.

Me: I'm just wondering if you feel that kind of relaxation where you just don't... you know, you just feel like you're floating and you just don't have a care in the world. You ever feel like that sometimes?

50

HELLO, SCAMMER
THE PATRICIA SERIES

BC: Um... Sir, I'm sorry, I'm at work so I don't have that type of feeling. But I'm looking to speak to Patricia Nelson – Patricia A. Nelson. Is she available?

Me: Would you like me to be Patricia? Cuz when I'm in this state I can be anybody you'd like me to be.

BC: (confused pause)
Okay, Sir, I'll try back...

Me: I'll get Patricia for you. One moment, please.

(pause – change voice to very deep, gruff, annoying...)

MMmmmm THIS IS PATRICIAAAAAAAAA! HOOOOW CAN I HELLLLLP YOU?

BILL COLLECTOR:

(trying not to laugh):
Okay, Sir, I'll call you back at another day. Thank you. Have a good day.

THE PATRICIA SERIES #9
MIGRATING MONARCHS

BILL COLLECTOR:

(Not recorded: This call may be monitored or recorded for quality assurance.)

Me: I don't want quality assurance.
Can we dispense with that part?

LISTEN
CD 1, TRACK 14

BC: (tersely): I'm calling to speak to Patricia Nelson.

Me: I'm sorry, can we talk about cats?

BC: What was that, sir?

Me: I'm sorry, who is this?

HELLO, SCAMMER

THE PATRICIA SERIES

BC: My name is Victoria and I'm calling to speak to Patricia Nelson.

Me: [pretend racking my brain]: Victoria, Victoria... Now who are you with again?

BC: I'm with Monarch _____. Is this a good phone number for Patricia Nelson?

Me: Is that monarch like as in the butterfly?

BC: Correct.

Me: That's crazy! You know about monarchs, about how they migrate and stuff, like from Canada to Mexico every year??

BC: Yes.

Me: Isn't that WILD?

BC: Is this...?

Me: I just saw a documentary about monarchs and I just thought that was just the coolest thing I'd ever seen in the entire. Freaking. World. Don't you agree with me?

BC: Sure. So is this a good number for her..?

Me: So, do you guys recover monarchs then?

BC: Okay. Sir, have a wonderful day.

Me: Wait.

BILL COLLECTOR:

HELLO, SCAMMER
THE PATRICIA SERIES

THE PATRICIA SERIES #10
HOW TO SCARE OFF A TELEMARKETER

Me: What was that again? You want to talk to Patricia?

TeleMarketer:
  Yeah, is that a place of work, um..?

Me: I'll get Patricia. Just heads up though, she's in a little bit of a mood today.

TM: Okay.

Me: But that's pretty normal for her. Hang on.

(talking off phone): Hey, Patricia!

Me As Patricia:
  (off phone – feminine whimpers)

Me: (off phone): Phone for you.

"MAP": (off phone): I don't wanna talk.

Me: Come on, get the phone.

TM: I can call her sometime later, Sir, if she's not in the mood…

"MAP": (comes to the phone with heavy, irritable breathing):

WHAT DO YOU WANT ?!?!

TM: (shocked pause)

  Oh, my gawd.

"MAP": WHAT??

TeleMarketer:

LISTEN
CD 1, TRACK 15

HELLO, SCAMMER

ANDREA BELL

ANDREA BELL #1
BOCCE[1] TRANSLATOR

After giving up on Patricia, some debt collectors switched to calling the wrong number for "Andrea Bell". It didn't go well for them.

LISTEN
CD 1, TRACK 16

Debt Collector: Hello?
Me: Hello!
DC: Yes sir, good afternoon. My name is Messissito _____ I'm calling on a recorded line, I'm looking for Andrea Bell.
Me: Oh, you want to speak to Andi?
DC: Andrea Bell.
Me: Oh yeah, you want to talk to Andi. Yeah. I can get her but, a real quick question – you know she only speaks **Bocce**, right?
DC: I'm sorry?
Me: Do you speak **Bocce**?
DC: No, sir.
Me: Ok. Cuz she only speaks **Bocce**. But you're in luck because um, I'm her translator, and I was just here giving her a lesson, an English lesson, so I can translate for you if you'd like.
DC: Well, I will need a um power of attorney before I can speak with you.
Me: I'm sorry, I'll translate for you.
(off phone): Hey, Andi!
(I become "Andi"...)
"Andi": (in a weird, high-pitched voice, off phone) Dldldldloo!

1   Bocce – a fictional language from *Star Wars*.

HELLO, SCAMMER

ANDREA BELL

Me: (off phone): Hey, Andi, um.... Skibidiskuskskskabisksuskskskskskusksbidiska?
"Andi": Skuskuskskksskskskskkksbidisksuskusksaksuskskiskaw!
Me: Skibidiskawskukskuskawksksksksksksksksku awdoo?
"Andi": Dldldldldldoo!
Me: (back on phone): Ok. She says, "Hello."
DC: Have in mind sir that the only thing you're doing is setting yourself up to receive another call. Thank you very much for your time today.
"Andi": OoooOOoOooOoo! SkubidiskuskskuskbsussksksksbksussSKUSKUSKSKU…
Debt Collector:

Messissito did not call back. Though they did try again (in vain)…

ANDREA BELL #2
TELEMARKETER PURGATORY LINE

LISTEN
CD 1, TRACK 17

Debt Collector:
Yes, I'm looking for Andrea Bell.
Me: (in a very low, serious voice): Yes. Does this concern a **very serious matter**?

HELLO, SCAMMER

ANDREA BELL

DC: Uh, no sir. It just concerns a personal business matter.

Me: Oh, it's a business matter? Okay, tell you what. If you can hold for one moment we'll take you to our escalation line. Ok? Hold on just a moment, please. And please have your credit card ready.

(MUSIC): The debt collector is blasted with hoedown music.

Me: (different, super friendly voice!): Hello! Thank you for calling Andrea's escalation line! May I help you?

DC: Yes. I'm trying to get a hold of Andrea Bell, please.

Me: Oh yes, we can connect you to her regular line. We'll need to get your payment of $99 first, though. Would you like to pay with Visa or MasterCard?

DC: No, sir. This is, uh, Brandi _____. I'm speaking on a recorded line calling Ms. Andrea Bell about a personal business matter. I need to speak with her, please.

Me: We'd be glad to connect you with her. We just need to get your payment information first. It's only $99 to connect her with her main line. That's our service – and we can do that for you! Now, we understand that might impose a hardship on you, so we can also do installment payments if you'd like – $33 a month for 3 months. Would that be better?

DC: (pauses, getting perturbed): Okay. We're calling to speak with Andrea about a **personal business matter** that she has in our office. Is there any way you could connect me with Andrea, or is she an employee at your business?

Me: I'd be glad to connect you! But we have to get the payment first. I tell you what…

DC: Okay sir, thank y…

Me: …We do offer a cash discount of 3% if that would help things out a little bit. What you can do is just put it in an

HELLO, SCAMMER

ANDREA BELL

	envelope and mail it to us. In the meantime 'til we get there we'll just hold the line for you. Would you prefer to do it that way?
DC:	(pause) No, sir. I just prefer to speak with Andrea. I'm not exactly sure what you're needing a payment for. If she's not there, I'd be glad to leave a message…
Me:	Well, this is the **escalation line**.
DC:	…or I'm gonna end the phone call.
Me:	This is the escalation line. We need to get your payment first.
DC:	Escalation for what, sir?
Me:	Well, you said this was a very important business matter. This is the business matter line that you've reached. It's an interim line, kinda like purgatory.
DC:	(pause) Okay, not exactly sure what you're talking about. What I'll go ahead and do is just notate down to remote this phone number from her personal business matter. (facetiously): And you do have a great day.
Me:	Well, that's great! Can I still get your payment info, though?
DC:	Uh, no sir. You have a great day now!
Me:	(more facetiously friendly): Oh, okay. You too!
DC:	Mmmm….bye bye.
Me:	Byyyeee!

(MUSIC): Telemarketer gets a second blast of more hoedown.

DEBT COLLECTOR:

HELLO, SCAMMER

PROPERTY BUYERS

One day I started receiving calls from property buyers interested in homes that weren't mine. It's unknown how my number got attached to them, but I am *so* happy they did. These scammers typically target poor homeowners in impoverished neighborhoods with low-ball offers (50-60% market value, or lower) in hopes of catching them in desperate need of cash. Property buyers can then quickly flip the property for a tidy profit. They target hot markets in more penurious neighborhoods where these homeowners may not know the current market value of their homes. To illustrate, one of the (redacted) addresses targeted in this book has an approximate value of $300k, while the property buyer offers only $115k[1]. I drove by this and others houses myself and found that they are indeed in poorer neighborhoods. By running interference for them, did I save some poor family from losing their home? Who knows? But here's what we do know: we shall have no mercy on these scammers.

GRANDMA!

LISTEN
CD 1, TRACK 18

Me: Hello?

Property Buyer:
(female voice): Hello?

Me: Hello?

PB: Hi, I'm looking for Patricia _____.

Me: Patricia? Yes?

PB: I'm sorry?

Me: Yeah, Patricia?

PB: Yeah.

Me: Uh huh.

PB: Is she available?

Me: Yeah, I'm Patricia.

PB: (confused pause) Oh, hi. Ahhh... No worries. This is just very quick. My name is Emma, and...

---

1   "Let Me Hear Your Sexy Voice"

HELLO, SCAMMER

PROPERTY BUYERS

Me: I love that name.

PB: You do?

Me: Emma?

PB: Uh huh.

Me: Yeah, that's my grandma's name. I love that name.

PB: (laughs) No. I am one of the local buyer in the area and I was just want to know if you're selling your property at _____ Drive?

Me: You know what's weird? You sound just like my grandma.

PB: Whyyyy?

Me: Your voice! It sounds... wait. **You're my grandma**!

PB: (laughs) No, sir. I'm just really interested in your property. Is that for sale?

Me: Grandma, you promised you'd bring cookies over today. Instead you went over to work.

PB: (laughs – long pause)

Me: You *promised*!

(pause)

PB: I.... well. Thank... thank you so much for your time though.

Me When do I get the cookies?

PROPERTY BUYER:

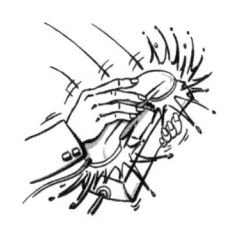

59

PROPERTY BUYERS

HELLO, SCAMMER

VERY SUPERSTITIOUS

Another property buyer called. Before she could finish her spiel we got disconnected. She kindly called back, which is where we pick it up. Another call where we get a scammer to say ridiculous things...

Me: (in a high, lispy voice): Hellos?

PROPERTY BUYER: Hello! Hi, Miss Jones, this is Jasmine. I really do apologize if our call got disconnected.

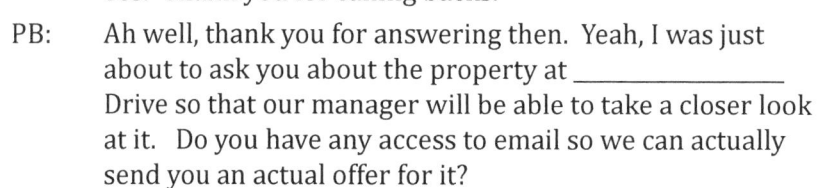

Me: Yes, we got disconnected I'm afraid. Yes. Thank you for calling backs.

PB: Ah well, thank you for answering then. Yeah, I was just about to ask you about the property at _____ Drive so that our manager will be able to take a closer look at it. Do you have any access to email so we can actually send you an actual offer for it?

Me: Yes, but as I was telling you, you see, today's Thursdays. I'm very, very superstitious, you see, and we can't do any deals on Thursdays because it will be 1,000 years of bad luck for you and for me! Do you understand?

PB: ...on Thursday? And if you don't mind me asking, like how much is the estimated price for your property so that I could actually give a heads up to our manager about this one?

Me: Well ma'am you see, we cannot do any deals or talks about this today because there's a curse on Thursdays on talking about these things. But you can help me lift ze curse. Can you help me, please? And then we can talk about it.

PB: (confused pause) So when will be the best day and time frame that we'll be able to give you a call back for this one?

LISTEN
CD 1, TRACK 19

HELLO, SCAMMER

PROPERTY BUYERS

Me: You can do it today, but you just must help me lift ze curse. Will you just say this after me, please? And the curse will be lifted.
You see...

PB: Ooooo-kay?

Me: ...my great, great Aunt Percy, she was a witch! She puts a curse on Thursdays. But we know how to lift ze curse now. So if you just say these things we can lift ze curse.

PB: Okay.

Me: Say it with me:
> *Mercy, mercy*
> *Great Aunt Percy*

PB:
> **Mercy, mercy**
> **Great Aunt Percy**

Me: Yes, yes!..
> *Be there now*
> *No more curse-y*

PB:
> **Be there now**
> **No more curse-y**

Me: Yes! Yes, yes! Say it again, please. Ze curse is lifting. It is working!

PB: (silence)

Me: Hellos?

PROPERTY BUYER:

HELLO, SCAMMER

PROPERTY BUYERS

BOOGER GHOULS

LISTEN
CD 1, TRACK 20

Me: Hello?
Property Buyer: Hello?
Me: Hello?
PB: This is Alex, sir. I'm looking for Mr. Jones.
Me: Jones? Yup.
PB: I'm just reaching out to see if you might be interested in a cash offer on your property?
Me: Yeah! Yeah, I'd be really interested in that.
PB: The property on _____ Drive?
Me: Yes, yes. Your timing is <u>perfect</u>. We were just talking about selling it.
PB: Alright, sir. Do you have a number in mind you'd like to have for this property?
Me: Yeah, we'd probably make a really good deal on it. Um. One caveat about it, though. You know this house in haunted, right?
PB: I'm sorry?
Me: This house is haunted. Are you ok with that?
PB: The one on _____ Drive?
Me: Yup, yup. It's haunted. It's got ghosts.
PB: (surprised): Okay?
Me: Are you okay with that?
PB: Yes.
Me: Okay great! What they usually do is they haunt you at night while you're asleep, and they like, pick your nose while you're sleeping. We call them **Booger Ghouls**.
PB: That's cool.

HELLO, SCAMMER
PROPERTY BUYERS

Me: Or **Snot Specters**.

PB: Mm-huh.

Me: You okay with that?

PB: Yeah.

Me: Okay! Excellent.

So I think what we should probably do though is you should come over and just try a little nap first, to make sure that it doesn't freak you out too much. Cuz what'll happen is then, we wanna make sure we don't get sued for non-disclosure of specters. You know what I'm saying?

PB: Uh-huh.

Me: Yeah. And then, so while you're drifting off to sleep, you may kinda feel like a little cold finger like going up your nose. Just relax! Just relax.

PB: Mmm-huh.

Me: That's just a Booger Ghoul digging around in there. And then when you wake up probably your nose will be all nice and clear. It's actually not all that bad really.

PB: Yeah?

Me: Yup.

PB: That sounds like a nice idea.

Me: Yeah?

PB: I'll come over.

Me: Okay yeah! So you'll come over, and just try a little half-hour nap. We got a really comfy couch for you. And then after you experience the Booger Ghouls, if you're still cool with it, we can probably make a great deal on it.

PB: Okay, perfect.

Me: Awesome.

PB: Okay.

Me: When do you want to come by?

HELLO, SCAMMER

PROPERTY BUYERS

PB: Whenever you're ready.

Me: Okay. Wanna come by tomorrow at like 2 o'clock?

PB: Okay, perfect.

Me: Awesome.

PB: All right.

Me: I'll see you then.

PB: Okay.

Me: Bye!

PROPERTY BUYER: HANG UP

O, to be a fly on the wall when this property buyer showed up at this house saying he was there to nap with Booger Ghouls.

REVERSE SURVEY

Q: When a property buyer scammer calls, how many pointless questions can you ask before he hangs up?
A: A LOT.

Picking up here after the initial pleasantries, telling him I would be interested in selling...

PROPERTY BUYER:
Okay. That's great, sir. Would it be the property at _____ Drive?

Me: Yeah, could be that one. We might want to sell that one.

PB: Okay.

Me: You want to buy it?

PB: Well I'm going to go ahead and get some

LISTEN
CD 1, TRACK 21

	information from you. Okay..?
Me:	Yeah.
PB:	...regarding this matter.
Me:	Can I get some information though from you first?
PB:	Absolutely! Go ahead.
Me:	What's your name?
PB:	My name is Alex.
Me:	Alex? Yeah. That's a pretty cool name. I like that name.
PB:	Yeah.
Me:	Yeah. How old are you?
PB:	I'm 24.
Me:	Okay. Yeah, you're just getting started at this. You sound pretty good, though! Yeah, you sound experienced.
PB:	I'm... so-so.
Me:	Yeah.
PB:	Actually I'm just gonna get some information for my acquisition manager and import it over to him, and he's going to go ahead and get you an offer. Okay?
Me:	But I'm still getting information from you, though.
PB:	That's fine.
Me:	Yeah. What are your like, what are your hobbies?
PB:	Uhh, I like playing soccer.
Me:	Yeah?
PB:	Umm, and going to the gym.
Me:	Yup.
PB:	Uhh, okay so...
Me:	And then, I'm still gathering some information. What are your favorite colors?

HELLO, SCAMMER

PROPERTY BUYERS

PB: Uh, turquoise.

Me: That's nice! That's unique.

PB: Black and turquoise.

Me: Yeah?

PB: Okay, so address at _____ Drive?

Me: Hang on a second. Do you have any bad habits? Like smoking, or like… I dunno. Like picking like toenail cheese or something like that?

PB: I'm sorry. Beg your pardon?

Me: Do you have any bad habits we should know about?

PB: Mmmm… not that I can think of.

Me: I mean, we'll hold this in confidence.

PB: Sometimes I can speed.

Me: Do you? You speed sometimes?

PB: I speed, yeah.

Me: Do you pick your toenails in public or anything like that?

PB: Mmmm… no.

Me: Okay. That's good.

PB: No, nothing like that.

Me: Yeah. Lice? No lice?

PB: Sorry?

Me: Do you have lice?

PB: Life?

Me: LICE. Like in your hair.

PB: Lice in my hair?

Me: Yeah.

PB: I don't.

Me: That's good to know.

PB: Last time I checked I didn't.

HELLO, SCAMMER
PROPERTY BUYERS

Me: Yeah.

PB: Sir um, so let's go ahead and, do you wanna go ahead and continue, sir?

Me: Oh yeah, yeah. Totally. Yeah. Do you?

PB: Well, I mean, it's up to you, sir.

Me: Yeah yeah! It's up to you, too.

PB: (pause)
All right, so that would be address, the property at _____ Drive?

Me: Yeah, yeah. Do you um… What kind of water to do you get when you go to the store? Do you get the fancy kind, or do you get the generic kind?

PB: Hmmm, honest I just get the generic kind.

Me: Yeah, it's probably just as good as the fancy kind, isn't it?

PB: Same. Yeah.

Me: Yeah.

PB: Ok so, do you have a cash offer for the property at _____ Drive, sir?

Me: Well, hang on. I'm still doing an interview here. Have you ever belonged to a cult?

PB: No, I have not.
So would that house be 3 bedrooms, 1 and ½ bathrooms and 1,300 square feet?

Me: What's the strangest book you've ever read?

PB: Hmmm… strangest book I've ever read?

Me: Yeah, yeah.

PB: Eeemmm, probably… If it's a strange book I'm not gonna read it. [chuckles]

Me: Oh yeah. Of course.
Do you have a back scratcher?

PROPERTY BUYERS

PB: Uhh, I don't.
Me: Okay.
PB: All right, sir. So do you know how much you're trying to get for the house, 3 bedrooms, 1 & ½ baths?
Me: Hang on. I'm just wondering, like...
PB: It's gotta be one to one, right? It's gotta be fair, man.
Me: Hold on, but I just gotta make sure we got the questionnaire we're going through here. So, we gotta make sure we got the right fit here for us. You know what I'm saying?
PB: Uh, okay.
Me: Yeah. How often to you change your bed sheets?
PB: I don't even see how... I don't see how that would work..? But okay.
Me: I'm just asking, how often do you change your bed sheets?
PB: A month. Every month.
Me: Okay. You might want to up that to like every week or so. But maybe you're pretty clean.
PB: Yeah, I'm hardly home. So..
Me: Okay, okay. So you sleep other places. I get it.
PB: (confused): Yeah.
Me: Do you have dust allergies? Are you allergic to dust?
PB: Uhh, no.
Me: Okay.
PB: Yeah well, I mean, yeah. I guess?
Me: Yeah? You do? Okay.
PB: Who isn't?
Me: It's kind of a dusty house. That's what I'm saying.

HELLO, SCAMMER
PROPERTY BUYERS

PB: So do you know how much you're trying to get in cash for the house?

Me: Yeah, the cash? Yeah. Do you usually pay cash or card for things, or check? Or how do you do it?

PB: (pause)... okay. Mr. Jones?

Me: Yeah?

PB: Can you please tell me how much you're trying to get for the house?

Me: Hang on. I'm still going through my questionnaire. Here.

PB: All right. How long is this going to take?

Me: I dunno. We go through this with every one of our buyers, potential buyer.

PB: Am I meeting the preliminary criteria?

Me: You're doing pretty good. You're doing pretty good. You know, we do have a lot of buyers, but we want to screen out the people that are maybe not good fits.

PB: I appreciate your willingness to... uh. I appreciate you being so intrigued in...

Me: Yes. It is.

PB: ...I dunno, my life, I guess.

Me: Yeah. Mmm huh.

PB: I'm going to go ahead and release the call, okay, Mr. Jones?

Me: Do you use a handkerchief or Kleenex?

PB: Have a great day, okay?

Me: Handkerchief or Kleenex? Which one do you use?

PB: Kleenex.

Me: Okay. Handkerchiefs are a little classier. You might want to...

HELLO, SCAMMER

PROPERTY BUYERS

PB: Sir, you have a great day, okay? I appreciate you taking your time to speak to me, all right?

Me: Get the embroidered kind of handkerchiefs with your initials on them.

PB: Have a great day.

Me: Yeah. Try those.

PB:

HELLO, SCAMMER

PHONE JEOPARDY!

PLAYING *PHONE JEOPARDY!* #1
WITH MANNY THE TELEMARKETER

TELEMARKETER:
(automated calling phone "bloop" sound)
Hello?

LISTEN
CD 1, TRACK 22

Me: Hello?

TM: Hi! This is Manny _____ from the promotions department of the _____, here to help you claim your complimentary cruise for two. How are you?

Me: Very well! So this is Manny?

TM: Yes, sir.

Me: Manny, thank you for calling PHONE JEOPARDY! Our categories today are...

    BEHAVIOR
    BEHAVIORS FOR SURVIVAL
    SURVIVING SEASONAL CHANGES
    SOCIETAL BEHAVIOR
    SEXUAL, ASEXUAL AND OTHER

Are you ready to play, Manny?

TM: (silence)

Me: Hello, Manny?

TM: (silence)

Me: Manny?

TM: (silence)

Me: (softer): Manny?

HELLO, SCAMMER

PHONE JEOPARDY!

TM: (silence)

Me: (whispering): Manny?

T‍ELE‍M‍ARKETER:

PLAYING *PHONE JEOPARDY!* #2
WITH DAN THE TELEMARKETER

T‍ELE‍M‍ARKETER:

    I was looking for Mr. Rue.

Me: Actually you have called PHONE JEOPARDY! It's just like the TV show except you play it on the phone. Today's categories are...

    BEHAVIOR

    BEHAVIORS FOR SURVIVAL

    SURVIVING SEASONAL CHANGES

    SOCIAL BEHAVIOR

    SEXUAL, ASEXUAL AND OTHER

Please pick a category!

LISTEN CD 1, TRACK 23

TM: BEHAVIOR for 500.

    (Telemarketer plays along. What a sport!)

Me: BEHAVIOR for 500. The answer is... Instinct as soon as they've been born.

TM: (pauses, thinking): Instinct as soon as they've been born... Hmmm. Human being..?

VERY LOUD BUZZER: BZZZZZZZZZZ!

Me: 5 seconds. Oh, I'm sorry. The correct question is: "Innate behaviors come from?" "Innate behaviors come from?" Okay, 500 bucks in the hole. All right, try again.
TM: I'll take BEHAVIOR for 700, Pat. It is Pat?
Me: That's correct. I'm sorry, what is your name again, sir?
TM: My name is Dan.
Me: Dan! Thank you for playing. Okay. We can get your for 400, though. BEHAVIOR for 400. The answer is...
TM: BEHAVIOR for 400!
Me: Behaviors that develop through experience from observing the actions of other animals.
TM: Is that the answer, or is that a...?
Me: I'm sorry, it needs to be in the form of a question.
TM: I'll have to pass.

VERY LOUD BUZZER: BZZZZZZZZZZ!

Me: I'm sorry. "What are learned behaviors?"

HELLO, SCAMMER

PHONE JEOPARDY!

TM: This is fun. I appreciate your, your... (laughs) I appreciate you making my morning a little better. Thank you Mr. Rue. You're awesome.

Me: Behaviors that develop without depending on learning or experience.

TM: Ummm... Very good. You win. Thank you.

        VERY LOUD BUZZER: BZZZZZZZZZZ!

TeleMarketer:

HELLO, SCAMMER

CHARITY CALLS

Who knows if these callers are from legitimate charities or not? We shall assume they're scammers until proven otherwise

VERSTEHEN BETTER

Me: (Thick German accent): Hallo?

TeleMarketer:

Hi, Mark!

Me: Ja?

TM: Hi, this is Wendy _____ with quick blessing, calling for the state troopers. How are you doing today, sir?

Me: Ahhh. Ausgezeichnet. Ja, very gut. Ja!

TM: Great. I was actually calling you today to thank your friends and family that support all the children. Actually goes a long way to provide them teddy bears – I'm sure you've seen our patrolmen at the scene of an accident just so the kids do have something to squeeze and hold onto until ambulances arrive. And we've actually pledged tremendous support of child abuse centers. Now we're just making sure that we can count on your support and mail you this year's envelope, if that's ok with you, sir?

Me: Ahhhh, so, ummm. Mein, um, Englisch not so gut. So could you please, ummm, start over and speak very uhh, uh slowly? Und um, umm, buchstabieren... ah, spell each word, please?

TM: Okay, ummm... We were actually calling you today to thank you, friends and family here...

Me: Can you please SPELL each word? Please? So I can, ahh, aufschreiben.... um, write down, write it down? Und then I can um... verstehen – ah, understand better. Ja?

HELLO, SCAMMER

CHARITY CALLS

TeleMarketer:

RIP VAN AX, EXS, ACHES..?

TeleMarketer:
Hello Ross!

Me: (Lethargic): Hello?

TM: Hi, this is a manager with "A.C.S." How may I help you?

Me: Oh, you're with **ax**?

TM: This is... (confused) This is Shawnee, the manager with A.C.S.

Me: Oh good! You're with **ax**. Yeah, you're with ax?

TM: With ax?

Me: Yeah. A.C.S. It's pronounced "ax," right?

TM: No.

Me: It's not? Oh.

TM: It's an acronym.

Me: Is it pronounced "Icks," "Ax," "Aches"...?

TM: (impatiently): A.C.S. is an acronym for Associated Community Services.

Me: Oohhh. But how do you pronounce the acronym?

TM: It's not pronounced. It's an acronym.

LISTEN
CD 1, TRACK 25

76

HELLO, SCAMMER

CHARITY CALLS

Me: Oh, it's like a symbol? Like Prince?

TM: Abbreviation.

Me: Yeah? You don't pronounce it like that?

TM: No.

Me: I'm really confused. I just woke up. What year is it?

TM: It is 2017.

Me: No freakin' way!!

TM: Do you have a question or concern, sir?

Me: Yeah! I wondered what year it is. But um.

TM: It's 2017!

Me: That freaks me out. No way...

How did that happen??

TM: (ignoring my shock): We were calling on behalf of the united breast cancer foundation to see if we can count on your support for these women in need.

Me: Wait. What day is it? Is it... What day is it?!

TM: (loudly into the phone): IT'S TUESDAY, SEPTEMBER 12TH.

Me: Whoooooah. How did that happen?

TM: (pause) I'm not sure, sir. But we were calling on behalf of the united breast cancer foundation...

Me: Yeah?

TM: ...and we're calling to see if you could support these women that are suffering breast cancer.

Me: Yeah, I'm just kinda freaked out right now.

TM: (strangely friendly): Okay, sir!

Me: What do you suggest I do about it?

TM: I'm not sure, but we could call you back at a later time. Is that okay?

Me: Oh. Yeah. What year will you call back?

TM: We'll just call you back at a later time.

HELLO, SCAMMER

CHARITY CALLS

Me: Like what, in a couple years or so?

TM: No, some time this week.

Me: Well. Probably won't be convenient. Like, if you could just try back in a few years? Um, might be, you know, I'll be less freaked out. And then you know.. Like 2020, 2021 – could we shoot for then?

TM: (confused pause)
Ok, sir. We'll call you back at a later time. Thank you for your time.

Me: Like in '28? Twenty...'28?

TM: Would you like to be placed on our do not call list?

Me: I don't know. Um. If we just set it for like 2028. 2027 would be okay, too. That would be fine if we do that.

TM: Okay, sir. You just have a great day. Okay?

Me: So 2027?

TM: Ok, sir. Have a great day. Bye bye.

Me: Is that when? Okay, cool. Talk to you in 2027.

TM: Mmmmkay. Have a great day. Bye bye.

Me: Okay. 2027 – we got a date.

TM: Okay! Thank you. Goodbye!!

Me: That's awesome. You guys are great.

TM: (pause)
Thank you.

Me: Well you're very welcome. You're really good with your thanks.

TM: Thanks. Have a great day. Bye bye.

Me: Okay. Bye bye.

TELEMARKETER:

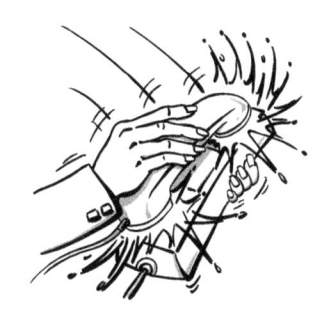

POSTSCRIPT

In 2021 the Tennessee Attorney General and Federal Trade Commission issued a press release announcing that Associated Community Services had been shut down as a sham charity organization. It was described as a " massive fundraising operation that collected more than $110 million through deceptive robocalls." It and various other defendants were each subject to monetary judgments of $110,063,843. "...the organizations for which they were fundraising spent little or no money on the charitable causes they claimed to support—in some cases as little as one-tenth of one percent. The defendants kept as much 90 cents of every dollar they solicited on behalf of the charities."

https://www.tn.gov/attorneygeneral/news/2021/3/4/pr21-09.html

https://www.ftc.gov/enforcement/cases-proceedings/162-3208/associated-community-services-inc

Bye, Scammers.

CHARITY CALLS

DONATION UNCERTAINTY

Automated Scammer Bot:

        How much would you like to donate?

Me: [intentionally exceeding their max donation threshold]: 500 dollars.

ASB: Could you repeat that, please?

Me: 500 dollars.

ASB: Yeah, and is that amount definitely comfortable for you?

Me: Pretty comfortable. Yup.

ASB: Okay. Hold on a sec.

LISTEN
CD 1, TRACK 26

Short pause while an Asian-accented telemarketer lady gets on the phone.

TELEMARKETER:

        Hi, this is Mary Williams, just jumping on to confirm you're helping with a 100 dollar donation.

Me: Hey, Mary. How are you?

TM: Hi! I'm doing good. How about you?

Me: I'm um.. a little uh antsy today. Um…

TM: I'm sorry?

Me: Yeah, feeling a little antsy.

TM: Are you comfortable with a 100 dollar donation?

Me: I don't know. Can we talk about this?

TM: I'm sorry?

Me: Yeah, I don't know. I… I'm feeling just… I think I'm comfortable, and then other times I don't feel like I'm comfortable. So can we talk this through?

HELLO, SCAMMER
CHARITY CALLS

TM: (pause)
Okay. Uh sir, I really do apologize, but I think we have a bad connection. I cannot clearly understand you.

Me: Yeah? I can hear you.

TM: Are you comfortable with a 100 dollar donation?

Me: Yeah, I'm comfortable at the moment. But... ok, now I'm not. So can we talk about it?

TM: Uh sir, we are having a bad connection right now. So again, are you comfortable with 100 dollar donation? Just yes or no.

Me: I'm not sure. I...I *think* so.
Yeah, yup, I am! Okay, right now I am! Yup, okay!

TM: Okay, great!

Me: Wait. Now I'm not. Now I'm not.

TM: Okay, what name should I put on your invoice? What's your last name?

Me: I suddenly got uncomfortable. Um, hold on.

TM: Ah. Mm-huh.

Me: Yeah. I think I'm gonna get comfortable again.
(pause)

TM: I'm sorry?

Me: Yeah... I'm getting comfortable again! Hold on. I wasn't sure for a second. Now I'm getting... it's coming back.
(pause)
Okay. Alright. I feel comfortable. Yeah.

TM: Okay, what name should...?

Me: Wait! No. I'm...

TM: (exasperated): Alright.

Me: ...I'm. Yeah, hold on. (pause)
Hey, Mary?

TM: Okay, what? I'm here.

Me: Okay, good. Thank you for...

HELLO, SCAMMER

CHARITY CALLS

TM: What is your full name? What is your last name?

Me: ...Thank you for being there for me.

TM: (silence)

Me: Can we just kind of like, can we talk through this a little bit more? So you're Mary?

TM: (pause) Okay. Uh sir, well my job here is to make sure that you are willing to donate to this organization. Okay?

Me: Yeah okay, okay.

TM: What is your last name?

Me: Yeah, no I just want to talk a little bit more, just to make sure that I'm comfortable with this. So like, when you get the money, do you put it in a piggy bank? Or like do you put it in like a sock? Or what do you do with the money when you get it?

TM: Hmm. Since you are not willing to donate, I will be removing your number off the list now and rest assured that you won't be receiving calls anymore.

Me: I'm very comfortable with the donation!

TELEMARKETER:

HELLO, SCAMMER

MEDICAL PRODUCTS

TELEMARKETER REUNION

TeleMarketer:

("bloop" sound)

Good afternoon, my name is Tomacina calling on behalf of medical alert systems. May I ask who I'm speaking with this afternoon?

Me: Oh. This is Jack. I'm sorry, who is this?

TM: Tomacina, sir.

Me: Tomacina?

TM: Yes.

Me: Huh... Tomacina.
I know you! Tomacina... Hey, it's me! It's Jack!

TM: Mmm-kay.

Me: From grade school!

TM: Right.

Me: Don't you remember??

TM: Are you interested in a medical alert system, sir?

Me: Wait wait wait wait wait! We know each other!

TM: *giggles*

Me: From uhhh... grade school!

TM: Which one? Maybe we do!

Me: Yeah! It was the one where we used to, well – it's probably more like uh...

TM: The one I went to is closed down. It was a really small one, so everybody who went there really, really knows each other. We're pretty close knit.

Me: Yeah?

TM: If you did, that's awesome! I'd love to keep in contact with you.

LISTEN

CD 1, TRACK 27

HELLO, SCAMMER

MEDICAL PRODUCTS

Me: Yeah??

TM: What state was that?

Me: Gosh. You know, we moved when we were so young.

TM: Oh, you would know the state. *giggles*

Me: Oh, would I?

TM: A very small state.

Me: Oh, was it?

TM: You would know it and the school.

Me: Huh. Well, I bet we know each other then.

TM: Okay! You don't sound like you're from up north. (does a Boston accent): You don't have that "Nawwthern" accent.

Me: Maybe not anymore.

TM: Yeah. This would be a town that you would know very well.

Me: Oh really?

TM: Mmm huh.

Me: So what have you been doing since then?

TM: Are you interested in a medical alert today? I don't usually get into my personal stuff, but... *giggles*

Me: Oh. Meh.

TM: It's a lot. A LOT. A lotta information! (laughs)

Me: Oh, is there? There's a whole lotta stuff that's happened?

TM: Yeah.

Me: Oh okay.

TM: Just like you, I'm sure.

Me: Yeah, yeah.

TM: As we grow and age, a lot happens. Family, children, grandchildren. You know?

Me: Grandchildren? Wow.

TM: *sniffles* Yeah.

Me: Huh. Okay. Well, good talking to you again!

HELLO, SCAMMER

MEDICAL PRODUCTS

TM: *laughs* You too! Enjoy your day!

Me: All right, bye!

TeleMarketer:

   Bye bye!

HANG UP

MEDICAL PRODUCTS

TELEMARKETER MEETS THE MUMBLER

TeleMarketer:
    ("bloop" sound) _____ health advisors, this is Sierra and I'll be assisting you today. May I ask who I'm speaking with?

Me: (in a low-key, mumbling voice)… Yeah, hey uh. This is uh uh, R-R-Roger.

TM: How are you today, sir?

Me: I'm ymlyahmodh. Yaw.

TM: Yeah?

Me: Mmmm… yaw.

TM: *giggles* I wanted to thank you for your interest in this revolutionary new medical approach to pain relief.

Me: Myeeeaw.

TM: And the fact is, sir, that over 50 million Americans suffer from physical pain on a daily basis.

Me: Ohhh yaaaw?

TM: And many of them don't know where to turn for relief.

Me Yawwww.

TM: Many of these patients who are suffering from pain have been looking for an effective but healthier alternative to the prescription pain pills that contain addictive narcotics.

Me: MMmmmawww.

TM: And now there's a great non-narcotic solution to relieve your pain, and it is completely paid for by your health insurance provider.

Me: Mmmm yawww!

TM: So what type of pain do you suffer from?

HELLO, SCAMMER

MEDICAL PRODUCTS

Me: Aww um, well um… Yaw. The pain is maoooo mliblty in the meqwuity when you transtransfer in the phagggon phaa in the sannfford and the fee. Can.

TM: (confused pause)
I'm sorry?

Me: Awww I'm sorry. Lemme repeat that again. The… the mouthaliblllty k-qwekquity in the since m-muuutransfer in the pisease. And that's the problem.

TM: (pause) Oh, ok. Ummm… Can you repeat that one more time?

Me: Oh sure, yeah. It's the the amouthalibitlllyt and the transfer and the ummmmm, the propteryum in spectaties min duh code. Is that, is that clearer to you?

TM: No, I still didn't get that.

Me: Hmmm.

TM: Is sounds like you're mumbling.

Me: Oh, I'm sorry. Lemme try… um, the problem is that when I go in the maomiablfty in equity and mouth tonsonsun. You got it?

TM: Are you trying to joke with me?

Me: Awww no.

TM: Is your name Mark?

Me: This is a very serious—matter.

TM: Okay, Mark. Well *laughs* I, I think you're trying to joke with me and it's hilarious. I'm rolling over laughing. Um…

Me: Mmmmnot funny.

TM: *laughs* Yeah, you should be a comedian. Do you do standup?

Me: Mmmmmmmmwellll ya know, in the mmmweekends annnnd mmmmfridays and mmmsaturdays and…

TELEMARKETER:
(*hysterically laughs*)

HELLO, SCAMMER

CREDIT CARD CALLS

All right, all right bro! I got you!

HANG UP

* This telemarketer was intrigued enough by this interaction that she called me back within a minute.

SHOULD I PRESS "1"?

Me: Yeah, hello?

TELEMARKETER:
(Asian accent): Yes. Can you hear me?

Me: Yes! I can hear you quite well.

TM: Okay. So... I say, I believe you pressed "1" to get a services on your credit card. Is that correct, sir?

Me: Oh, I pressed "1" a whole bunch of times. Should I...?

TM: What did you..?

Me: Okay, I'll press 1. Hang on. (I press "1" – BEEP)

TM: Ooo-kay.

Me: Did you get that "1"?

TM: Do you need credit card...?

Me: Dude, do I need to press "1" again?

TM: Yes, sir.

Me: Hang on. (BEEP) Did I get it right?

TM: One more time.

Me: Did I get it right?

TM: Mmmm-huh.

Me: Okay. Should I press "1"?

LISTEN
CD 1, TRACK 29

HELLO, SCAMMER

CREDIT CARD CALLS

TM: Press "1"?

Me: Yeah (BEEP)
Okay.

TM: Okay. Now press "2".

Me: Okay. (I press "2" – BEEP)

TM: Oooo-kay. And one more thing, sir – do you have a credit card?

Me: Um, yeah. Do I need to press "1" again?

TM: Uhhhhh... Shove it up in your "azz." On your telephone.

Me: What's that?

TM: I'm saying, shove it up in your "azz."

Me: Oh. Which part?

TM: In your "azz."

Me: In my "azz"?

TM: Yes.

Me: Huh. Like in my "A-Z"?

TM: Yes.

Me: Huh. I don't, I don't have an "azz."

TM: Okay. Let me explain you that you're a mother_____er. Go and f___k yourself mother_____er. Suck my d__k and die.

Me: Should I press "1" again?

TeleMarketer:
Sh__t!

HELLO, SCAMMER

CREDIT CARD CALLS

BETTER CARD RATE

Yet another "lower your credit card rate" scam call from somewhere in India…

LISTEN
CD 1, TRACK 30

Me: Hello?

TeleMarketer:
 (thick Indian accent): Yes?

Me: Yes!

TM: Wheech card do you have, sir?

Me: I've got a Sam's card.

TM: Sam's Club?

Me: Yeah, Sam's Club card, huh huh. And I got a library card, aaaaand I've got a um YMCA card, aaaaand I think I've got a way old Blockbuster card somewhere…

TM: ooh.

Me: …even though Blockbuster's been out of business for a long time! I just keep the card around just for kicks. So can you do a better rate on the Blockbuster card?

TM: Yeah, vee are going to rrrdeeduce down the interest drate on all of your crdedit card less than thrdee pair-cent for the lifetime, ok?

Me: Really??

TM: Yeah.

Me: You can do better than 3 percent on the Blockbuster card?

TM: Yes.

Me: You can?

TM: Can you verdify me with the ex-pyre-ation date of your crdedit?

90

HELLO, SCAMMER

CREDIT CARD CALLS

Me: Yeah, I think the Blockbuster card expired in... I think like 1998, 1999. Something like that.

TM: Ok, and you have your Sam's Cldub card with you?

Me: Yeah, the Sam's Club card. Yeah, mmm-huh.

TM: You verdify the expiration of your Sam's Cldub?

Me: I haven't been there in a long time. Cuz I didn't get a good enough rate! So I think that one expired like in 2005, 2006. Something like that. Yeah.

But I would like a better rate on it!

TM: Ok. The card number? What is the card number?

Me: On Sam's Club? I don't know, I don't have it in front of me.

TM: Can you've had yourd card handy? I'm holding the line for'd ydou.

Me: Oh, you are!?

TM: Yes.

Me: Ok. I'll have to go to the next state because I think it's back where I used to live. So can you hold for like, I dunno, it's gonna take me about 3 hours to get there, 3 back... like six hours. Can you hold for SIX HOURS?

TELEMARKETER:

HELLO, SCAMMER

CREDIT CARD CALLS

YEAH!

What happens when about the only thing you respond with is... "Yeah!"?

LISTEN
CD 1, TRACK 31

TeleMarketer: (heavy Asian accent): You want to get yourself a lower interest rate on your existing credit cards, correct?

Me: Hmm. Um I think... yeah. Yeah!

TM: Ok, no problem! And it shows that, sir, for past 6 to 8 months you have been making your payments on time, you never missed it, in fact you always try to pay more than the minimum payments, correct?

Me: Yeeeeaaaahhhh. Yeah, yeah, yeah! Uh-huh, uh-huh!

TM: Exactly.

Me: Uh-huh!

TM: Exactly! For that reason, sir, you are "callified" by the Experian sir because Experian is the one who will look after your payment history and provide you the credited score.

Me: Yeah.

TM: So that Experian is the one who picked up your profile for the review to bring down the interest rate on all of your existing Visa, Master, Discover and American Express pair, okay?

Me: I LOVE those guys! Yeah!!

TM: That's perfect. As your previous account summary shows, you still owe more than 4,000 approxi-mayte-lee basically between all your credit cards. Is that still accur-ate, sir?

92

HELLO, SCAMMER

CREDIT CARD CALLS

Me: Yeeaaah. Yeah, yeah, yeah!

TM: And the interest rate that you have been paying on your credit card are more than 10%, correct?

Me: Yeah... yeah yeah yeah!

TM: Exactly! And now, on behalf of your good payment history and your good credited score, we are going to drop down your interest rate to less than 6%...

Me: Yeah?

TM: ...for the rest of your life, sir. Sounds good for you?

Me: YEAAAAHHH! Yeah yeah yeah yeah! Uh huh. Yeah.

TM: That's perfect. So let me know, sir, which credit card you use the most, you think your carry the major balance on? Would that be your Visa, Master, or Discover? Which one is that?

Me: Lemme think a minute...

Ummm, yeah. Uhhhh, yeaaaah yeahyeahyeahyeahyeah. Yeah...

It might be the Master. But it might be the Visa, too. Soooo, yeah. Yeah. Yeah.

TM: What I'm going to do next sir is...

Me: Yeah.

TM: ...I'm going to simply pulling up account details for your satisfaction...

Me: Yeah.

TM: ...of my database, and I will let you know the exact balance you owe, the last payments you made, the new payments on your credit card, sir. So first of all can you grab your credit cards in your handy, and verify me the expiration date off your Visa card first of all for the verification purpose, please?

Me: Yeeeeeah. Yeah, hang on. I don't have it right with me here.

TM: Yeah, I'm holding the line for you. You take your time and grab your credit card, please.

HELLO, SCAMMER

CREDIT CARD CALLS

Me: Okay. How long are you going to hold for?

TM: Oh sir, whatever. You take the time.

Me: Whatever it takes?

TM: Yes, sir.

Me: Oh, that's great. Cuz I got to go like… Let's see, I trying to remember where the cards are. I think I left them at my parents' house. Um, I might have to wait until they get home later tonight. So—can we, can you hold for, you know, until, like, for 8 hours?

TM: But I can call you back in 8 hours, sir.

Me: Oh, you can?

TM: You don't have any credit card with you now?

Me: Yeeaaaahhh. Yeah. Lemme think about that. Hold on.

TM: Do you have any credit cards with you right now?

Me: Um… yeahhhh. Yeah yeah. Lemme think. Hold on…

Yeah. Ummm yeah. Yeahhhh. Uh uh. Yeah, ummm, uhhh… Mmmmmm yyyyyeah. Ahhh, yeah. Uhhhh… I'm looking. Hold on.

Yeah. Yeah. Yeahhhhh. Hold, I'm lookin. Yeaaah. Yyyyyyyyyeah. Yeah, yeah, yeah…

Oh yeah! Yeah yeah! Right here!

Oh wait.

No. no.

TELEMARKETER:

HELLO, SCAMMER

CREDIT CARD CALLS

MUTUAL FRIENDS

LISTEN
CD 1, TRACK 32

Me: Hi, how are you?
TELEMARKETER:
I'm good, sir.
Me: Yeah? What are you doin'?
TM: (Indian-sounding accent): Uh, I see that you're responding to get a lower interest rate on your exiting credit card.
Me: Oh, is that what you called about?
TM: Mmm-huh.
Me: Okay. Yeah? What else are you doing?
TM: Well, today we received your profile by major credit reporting bureau.
Me: You did?!
TM: "Peerian." Yes...
Me: Who?
TM: ...and it shows that...
Me: So "Peerian" sent it to you?
TM: Yes.
Me: I love Peerian. Peerian is one of my best friends. I love him. He's great. How do you guys know each other?
TM: Uh, it's a company, sir. Credit reporting bureau.
Me: No no, Peerian is my buddy. We went to grade school together.
TM: Umm. It could be your buddy as well.
Me: Oh really?! Okay. Did you guys go to school together, too, like college or something like that? Were you guys like fraternity brothers?
TM: Nnnnno.

95

HELLO, SCAMMER

CREDIT CARD CALLS

Me: You weren't? Oh. How did you guys know each other then?

TM: We are on "ExPEERIAN," the credit reporting bureau.

Me: Oh, **Peerian**?

TM: ... getting yourself confused with... Yeah.

Me: Oh, you're Peerian? Okay. Yeah, that's what I said – **Peerian**. Yeah.

(scammer tries to return to his script...)

TM: Being a consumer, you are paying your bills on time, you're never late with your payments. In fact, you always try to pay more than the monthly minimum payment. Is that correct?

Me: Did Peerian tell you that?

TM: I'm sorry?

Me: So Peerian told you that?

TM: No, I'm asking you. Is that correct?

Me: I'm asking, how did you know that? Cuz Peerian told you?

TM: No, no one told me. I'm asking...

Me: Oooohhh, he didn't? Okay, okay. I thought that like you and Peerian were tight. I thought you guys were really good buds. Cuz like, any friend of Peerian is a friend of mine. You know? And so like if he's cool with you, then I'm cool with you, too.

TM: Okay, so would you say that you make your payments on time? Your monthly payments?

Me: Um yeah. If Peerian says so. Did Peerian say so? He handles my stuff usually. Ask Peerian about that cuz he's got all that information. That's how good buds we are. I just say, "Hey Peerian, just take care of everything."

TM: Yes, but ummm... He didn't give me this information.

Me: Oh. He didn't?

TM: Do you, do you..?

HELLO, SCAMMER
CREDIT CARD CALLS

Me: I thought you said he gave you this information? So, wait, so you guys DON'T know each other?

TM: Mmmmm... no.

Me: Oh, you don't? Oh. Well, huh. That kinda changes things. Let's see if we got any other mutual friends maybe as well.

Mmmm... Do you know my buddy Randy?

TM: No. No Randy.

Me: You don't? You don't? Okay.

Do you knooooow..... Jamie? My friend, Jamie. Do you him?

TM: Last name?

Me: Smith. Jamie Smith. Do you know Jamie Smith?

TM: Nnnnnnnno.

Me: You don't? Let's think about this. Who else could you know... (pondering)
What about... Pat? Do you know Pat?

TM: Patrick?

Me: Yeah. Yeah yeah! Could be Patrick, too.

TM: Huh huh.

Me: You do?!

TM: Yeah, Patrick. I know a Patrick.

Me: Oh, do you? Cool, cool! So like, you guys have a long history?

TM: Mmmm, business relations.

Me: It's just business? Oh, okay.

TM: Uh huh.

Me: Cuz Pat knows like everything about me, too. You could ask him about that, your questions that you want answered. You wanna ask Pat? Get him on the phone! I tell you what, get him on the phone, we'll do a 3-way call. Then we can get everything going. How's that? Is that cool?

TM: Um, I don't have his number.

HELLO, SCAMMER

CREDIT CARD CALLS

Me: Oh, okay. I thought you were good friends with him. You can go get it if you want.

(telemarketer tries once again to get back on his script)

TM: Uhhh.... Anyways. So. I was saying that um, you make your payments on time, your monthly minimum payments?

Me: Yeah well, Pat would know.

TM: Ummm.. Who's Pat?

Me: Your friend. My friend. Patrick.

TM: Your friend, um?

Me: Yeah yeah! We're mutual friends, right? We just figured that out, right?

TM: Do you have number so I can get in touch with him?

Me: Yeah, let's see, um... You wanna call 257[1]...

TM: Uh huh.

Me: 333.

TM: 333?

Me: Yeah. 7826. 5...

TM: 7 8.

Me: ...9. And then you want to press the * button like 3 times.

TM: Uh huh.

Me: And then the # button once. And then wait 5 seconds and press # again. Okay?

TM: Okay.

Me: You wanna repeat that back to me? Okay?

TM: 257-337-826.

Me: 9.

TM: That's an extra digit.

Me: And then... No, you gotta put that in, too. And then you got

---

[1] 257 is not a real area code.

HELLO, SCAMMER

CREDIT CARD CALLS

the thing about the * ? You gotta press * . Tell me about the * button.

TM: It's 257-333-7826.

Me: 9.

TM: I'll go ahead and give Pat a call.

Me: 9. Yeah, 9. And then, did you get the * button thing, too? Can you tell me that again?

TM: (silence)

Me: Hello?

TeleMarketer:

HELLO, SCAMMER

CREDIT CARD CALLS

HANG ON FOR COOKING

A telescammer happened to call when I was reheating lunch in the microwave. I checked it every 5 seconds just for him.

LISTEN
CD 1, TRACK 33

TELEMARKETER:
(in a heavy Asian accent): Alright, so uh do you want lowered interest rates on your credit card?

Me: Oh yeah, totally! Yup.

TM: Perfect. Which card do you have with the major balance right now?

Me: Yeah. Hang on. Let me grab the card. Then I can tell you what's going on with that. Let's see if I can find it here—

(beeping sound of microwave buttons being pressed in the background)

But uh. Let's see. Hold on. You know what? I think—

(microwave fan whirrs to live in the background)

Let's see. I think my food is almost ready. Hang on just a sec here—

(microwave beeps in background as it finishes)

Yeah, you hear that? Hang on just a sec.

(microwave door opens in the background)

No, not quite. All right. Hold on.

(microwave door slams shut)

TM: Sorry?

Me: Hang on. Let me see. My food, I gotta put it back in the microwave for a few more seconds. Hang on just a sec.

(microwave buttons being pushed, fan starts, loud beeps.)

Okay, let's see if that did it now. Let's see.

HELLO, SCAMMER
CREDIT CARD CALLS

(sound of microwave door opening, plates sliding around)

I think, hmmm. Lemme try... How long do you gotta put shepherd's pie in the microwave, do you know?

(microwave door slams shut)

TM: Sir, I don't have to speak about your microwave. I'm asking you which card do you have with the major balance right now.

(microwave fan starts up)

Me: I know. But you called me right in the middle of cooking some stuff. So, I really want to talk to you about this...

(microwave beep beep beep)

...but I just gotta figure out how long you need to put this in the microwave. And I'm doing it like 5 seconds at a time. Is that..?

TM: So from 20 minutes, like from 5 minutes you're just putting things in your microwave?

Me: Yeah. Am I doing that wrong?

TM: Sir, you just do it all day...

(microwave door slams shut)

...you just keep the things and take it out and you just tell people to hold on, hold on gimme a second?

Me: Yeah. What was that again? The microwave...

TM: (getting impatient): Do you have the card??

Me: Um. Yeah, but hold on. I just gotta finish cooking my food here.

TM: Uhhh, sir. I cannot.

(microwave buttons being pushed)

Me: Oh, you don't?

TM: You repeat it a lot!

Me: I really want to talk about the card.

TM: You're on the call for 300 seconds, you can just check your

101

HELLO, SCAMMER

CREDIT CARD CALLS

---

        phone, as well.

              (loud microwave fan starts up again)

        (getting stressed): You're saying, "One second! One second!" and I'm here from 300 seconds!

Me: What's that?

              (microwave BEEP BEEP BEEP BEEP)

TM: What is that??

Me: What?

TM: (unintelligible)

Me: That's the microwave. You hear that beep? That's uh... hold on.

TM: SO WHAT SHOULD I DO ABOUT IT?!

Me: Well, just hold on. Cuz you know I'm just like...

TM: I cannot!

              (microwave door slams shut)

        Have a blessed day!

Me: Hold on!

              (microwave buttons being pushed)

        I'm gonna grab my card here...

TM: I cannoooooot!!!

Me: ...in just a second here.

TM: You're saying you're going to grab it, but you're not grabbing it!

Me: No, I'm gonna grab it...

              (microwave BEEP BEEP BEEP BEEP)

        You hear it? It keeps beeping. And I gotta tell you that I gotta check it every time it beeps to make sure...

TM: You keep holding for 5 minutes, then you can do it later!

HELLO, SCAMMER
CREDIT CARD CALLS

Me: (distracted): Yeah. There's um… Hold on. I don't want to overcook it. I don't want to undercook it. So I just want to make sure it's just right. And then I can grab my card…

TM: I want to make sure my job is right! Have a blessed day. Bye for now…

(microwave door opening and slamming shut)

Me: So you want to talk about the… I got my card here!

TM: No, I don't want to talk about anything.

Me: Yeah, you don't?

TM: I don't want to talk about anything.

Me: You want to talk about the card?

(loud microwave fan sound starts)

TM: No, I don't wanna.

Me: Oh, you don't wanna?
(BEEP BEEP BEEP)
I thought you called because you wanted to talk about the card?

TM: I called you for that! But you're telling me your recipes you're cooking so what should I do for your cooking? That's not my business!

Me: Yeah, but just hold on. But I thought maybe you could help me with the cooking.

TM: (desperately): I cannot hold on, sir! How long you're making me hold on? Did you ever notice your phone? Just have a look at your phone how many seconds it's been!

Me: Yeah, I don't know. I'm not looking at the phone cuz I'm looking at the food right now. So…

TM: All right, then have a blessed day! If you're cooking the food, have a blessed day!!

HELLO, SCAMMER

CREDIT CARD CALLS

Me: Yeah but, I got my card here though.
>(microwave door SLAMS shut)

TM: Which card is that?
>(door SLAMS shut again)

Me: Yeah. It's the one that's... Wait, hold on.
>(microwave buttons being pushed, loud fan)

There's another thing here with the microwave. Let's see if this is done.
>(BEEP BEEP BEEP BEEP)

Yeah...

TM: Which card do you have?

Me: It's the...

Hold on.
>(microwave door creaks open)

You know, it's not quite done yet. Hold on.

TELEMARKETER:

Have a...
>(SLAM)

...blessed day.

HELLO, SCAMMER

CREDIT CARD CALLS

π CARD

Female automated scammer bot:

> You now qualify for zero percent interest rates on all your credit card accounts! If you have completed this process or are not interested, press "3" now. Otherwise press "1" now to speak to our qualification department and complete the process! The qualification process can be completed in a few minutes!

LISTEN
CD 1, TRACK 34

You know I pressed "1."

Male automated scammer bot:

> Thank you for your response. We would now like to transfer you to a poll taker for just a few more questions. Please stay on the line.

"Bloop" sound – lots of yammering in the background. The scammer is obviously one of many in a large room fielding calls.

TELEMARKETER:

> (Asian accent): Account services, how are you doing today?

Me: I'm doing really good! How are you?

TM: Fine. And I believe you responding to get the lower rate, right?

Me: Yes, that's correct.

TM: So on behalf of your good credibility and your good payment history, today you getting lower rate from your credit card accounts, okay?

Me: Oh, fantastic! Great!

TM: So now for the qualification purpose on which credit card

105

HELLO, SCAMMER
CREDIT CARD CALLS

---

	do you think you owe more, Shawn? Is that your Visa card or your MasterCard?
Me:	I would say my MasterCard probably.
TM:	And how much do you owe on your MasterCard? Just give me a rough idea.
Me:	Oh gosh, I dunno. It's probably, ya know, 10,000 or more maybe. It's a lot. Can you help me with that?
TM:	And when does your MasterCard expire? Find me expiration date on your MasterCard.
Me:	Yeah, sure. It expires on, let's see, it'll be 10/20.
TM:	10/20?
Me:	Uh huh.
TM:	On the face of the card you will see the four-block number, starting with "5" the same card you have.
Me:	Yeah yeah, uh huh.
TM:	So what is the after that number?
Me:	Okay. Then it's, okay it's 3.1415…
TM:	No no NO!
Me:	… 92653589793. Do you want me to keep going[2]?
TM:	Sir, this not a card number! The card number is starting with 5!
Me:	Oooh. Okay. So you want a 5 first?
TM:	Yeah.
Me:	Okay. So the number is 5, and then 3.14159265…
TM:	Sirrrrr!
Me:	…3.
TM:	I think… I think you're trying to playing games with me.
Me:	Oohhh! Noooo no no. I'm sorry, that was my ***Pi (π) Card***! I'm sorry. Hold on. Let me get the right card here. Ummm… ok. Alright, you ready?

---

2   In case you didn't know, *pi* (π) is an infinite number.

HELLO, SCAMMER

CREDIT CARD CALLS

Silence except for the multitudinous background chatter of other scammers bleating, "Account services, how can I help?"

Me: Hello?

TM: Yeah yeah, I write down the number.

Me: Okay okay. It's **867-5309**...

TM: Oh my gawd. Okay, have a good day. Goodbye[3].

Me: Oh wait! I want a better rate.

TM: You give me credit card number! What do you think I'm stupid, huh?

Me: Well, noooooo. No. I want a better card rate! Ok?

TM: Verify me the card number, please, just verify me the number for the recorded line...

Me: Yeah, I'm sorry...

TM: ...starting with 5!

Me: ...sorry, that was my Jenny Card[4]. I'm sorry. Ok. So the number is, okay it's...

Number 9

Number 9

Number 9

Number 9

Number 9[5]...

TM: Oooo-kay.

Me: You got that?

TELEMARKETER:

---

3 Did he know the song, or only that it wasn't a credit card number?

4 In case you didn't know, Tommy Tutone's 1981 hit "867-5309" is also known as "Jenny".

5 Beatles "Revolution 9"

HELLO, SCAMMER

CREDIT CARD CALLS

XXX TELEMARKETER

In case you feel sorry for scammers, here is a prime example of why you shouldn't. Often times they are running pornographic phone lines alongside their other schemes. It's all the same people. Their civil tone is a thin veneer concealing their true nastiness. Watch what happens when he catches on to what I'm doing...

TeleMarketer:
(Asian accent): Thank you for calling card services, how are you doing today?

Me: (emulating his Asian accent and sales pitch): Hello, this is "Matt" with the card services.

TM: That's right.

Me: Yes, THIS is Matt with the card services! How are you today?

TM: All right. I'm good. And I...

Me: Yes, I believe you pressed "1" to get a lower interest rate.

TM: That's right.

Me: Yes!? How much debt credit card do you have?

TM: I have 5,000 dollars in my Visa card.

Me: Yes? Would you like a lower interest rate?

TM: That's right.

Me: Yes! How much lower would you like?

TM: I want... less than 5%.

Me: How about 4.99%?

TM: Is that good?

Me: Yes!

LISTEN
CD 1, TRACK 35

HELLO, SCAMMER

CREDIT CARD CALLS

"Bloop" sound, indicating someone else has come on the line. Pretty sure the telemarketer was preparing the "special audio" for me. Hearing it I acknowledge it...

Me: Welcome to card services!
TM: What I have to do?
Me: You must give your card number.
TM: All right, I have a Visa card. Just can you hold on? Let me grab my card.
Me: O-kkkkkkay!
TM: All right, hold on.
Me: O-kkkkkkay!

"Bloop" sound again

Me: Welcome to card services!
TM: All right. Sir, I will be right back.
Me: Okay!
TM: I have my card number.
Me: OKAY!
TM: It's... (reads off a card number, most likely stolen from one of their victims).
Me: And what is the expiration date?
TM: It's 9/20.
Me: And what is the number on the back?
TM: (reads the number).
Me: And what's the name on the card?
TM: The name on the card is Kate _____.
Me: Kate? How do you spell?
TM: K-A-T-E. Middle initial is K...

HELLO, SCAMMER

CREDIT CARD CALLS

(Note these people have no qualms about giving away a stolen card number freely to anyone in the world, even if it's just to mess with someone like me who is messing with them.)

At this point the telemarketer starts playing a pornographic recording of a girl with a seductive "bimbo voice"...

Girl Seductive Voice:
Thanks for calling!

Me: (puzzled): Yes??

GSV: Want me to send you a ssssexy pic of me? Press "1" now if you're over 18 to give your consent to receive a naughty XXX photo...

Over this recording the telemarketer starts making loud moaning, gyrating sounds of ecstasy...

TM: Aaaaaaah! AAAAAaahhhhhh! Yesssssssss!

Me: Oh??

Girl Seductive Voice continues:
...to go directly to the menu.

Me: Would she like a lower card interest rate, too?

TM: Oooooo yessss! YESSSSSS!

GSV: ...press "3" and the other HHHHOT girls here at 1-800-SEX-TALK will fulfill your *dirtiest* fantasies!

(Girl Seductive Voice recording ends).

TM: (smugly): All right, sir. Are you there?

Me: Yes. Yes. Does she want a lower interest rate, too?

TM: Did you enjoy that, sir?

110

HELLO, SCAMMER

CREDIT CARD CALLS

Me: Yes. Does she want a lower interest rate, too?
TM: Yes.
Me: Yes? Ok and uh…
TM: Do you have a big c__k?
Me: Yes!
TM: You have a big c____k, right?
Me: Yeeeeeeesss.
TM: I bet that's been around. And your mom is sucking my d____k, did you know that? And she's good in there when she lick my b_____s. So yes! AAAAAAHHHH, suck my d____!
Me: Yes?
TeleMarketer:

111

HELLO, SCAMMER

CREDIT CARD CALLS

SWEDISH CHEF

Following the theme of the previous call, this reveals scammers for who they really are – fetid folks. I did my best "Swedish Chef" impression from The Muppet Show for him. Strange, he didn't seem to get nostalgic at all...

**LISTEN
CD 1, TRACK 36**

TeleMarketer:
  Holding the line with card services. How are you doing today?

Me: (Swedish Chef voice):
  Ohhh, de hee dåy de credit card! Därumph.

           (pause)

TM: I believe you're responding to get a zero percent interest rate on your credit card accounts, is that correct?

Me: Yåwr! Oh de børk in de meat børk did de. Børk bork bork. Jå jå jå!

           (pause)

TM: Yeaaaah.
  Yesterday I was f___king your daughter side by kuzey and it's make me lots pleasure!

Me: Ohh? It's in de meatballs!

TeleMarketer:

HELLO, SCAMMER

CREDIT CARD CALLS

SPEBSNOKSKIG THE CAT (AND MY BIRTHDAY)

This telemarketer actually indulged me for a bit, tolerating my nonsense for a short bit without talking about his scam. But not forever.

LISTEN
CD 2, TRACK 1

TeleMarketer:
(Asian accent): Card services, how are you?

Me: Good! How are you?

TM: I'm pretty much fine, sir. Thank you for asking. I see that you're responding to get the lower interest rates on your credit card accounts, correct?

Me: That's correct.

TM: All right. Well on the basis of your good credibility and your good payment history, on which of the credit card you want to get the lower interest rate on, sir?

Me: Um. Can we talk about cats instead?

TM: Cats?

Me Yes.

TM: I'm sorry. I beg your pardon, sir. What did you say?

Me: Can we talk about cats instead?

TM: Cats instead?

Me: Cats.

TM: Cats? C-A-T-S?

Me: Yeah. "Meow."

TM: Oh, why??? (long, weird laugh): W-whoa.. hahahahahahahaha!

HELLO, SCAMMER

CREDIT CARD CALLS

	Ahhh, I got… Do you have cats?
Me:	Oh yeah. Yeah. Do you?
TM:	Which one you got?
Me:	The little fuzzy one.
TM:	Fuzzy one? Which one?
Me:	It's the gray one. Just so cute.
TM:	Got a name or no?
Me:	Yeah.
TM:	What is it?
Me:	**Spebsnokskig**.
TM:	Nokskig?
Me:	No, no. **Spebsnokskig**.
TM:	I got one right now as well for myself.
Me:	You do?
TM:	Yes! Yeah. His name is Graphite.
Me:	Graphite?
TM:	Graphite, yeah.
Me:	That's a nice name.

(long pause – din of many other scammers running their scripts in the background)

TM:	Anything else you want to talk about?
Me:	Yeah.
TM:	What?
Me:	It's also my birthday today.
TM:	Oh! Happy birthday to you! Well, may you have many, many more, sir.
Me:	Thank you! Could you…No one has sung me "Happy Birthday" yet today. Could you be the first to sing "Happy Birthday" to me?

114

HELLO, SCAMMER

CREDIT CARD CALLS

TM: (pause) Uuuuuummmmmmmm…

Me: Please??

TM: AAaaaahhhhh…..
Come on, mayne. You're putting me in a bad shoes now!

Me: Naw. I can't get down to business until… I just gotta get this, I mean… I'm just not feeling up for business until someone wishes me a "Happy Birthday" singing. Can you, please?

TM: All right. Only on one condition!

Me: Okay.

TM: Be true and be nice! Be honest, okay??

Me: Okay.

TM: Whatever I ask you, okay? Be honest and be true, okay?

Me: Oh yes!

TM: Do you have credit cards?

Me: I'll tell you about it after you sing Happy Birthday.

TM: Now I ask you first, be true, be honest. I'll ask you something, then I'll sing a Happy Birthday for you.

Me: Yeah?

TM: Guess what? All office complete are gonna sing Happy Birthday for you!

Me: Oh, you are!?!

TM: Yeah. Everyone is gonna sing Happy Birthday for you! We got 8, 10..? Yeah, 10 peoples on the floor, on the one floor where I am right now.

Me: (voice quivering): That's awwwesome.

TM: All of us!

Me: I'm gonna cry. I think I'm gonna cry!

TM: Don't cry now, cry after! When we sing it for you.

Me: Okay, that's really touching!

TM: Yeah!

HELLO, SCAMMER

CREDIT CARD CALLS

Me: Can you get them all together?

TeleMarketer:

Alright, go f__k yourself, motherf_____er!!!

HELLO, SCAMMER

CREDIT CARD CALLS

PERFECTLY BALANCED

LISTEN
CD 2, TRACK 2

TeleMarketer:

...that is the major balance on? Would that be your Visa card or the Master?

Me: Yes, what are you calling about again?

TM: Visa and MasterCard – which you have a larger balance?

Me: The Visa-MasterCard balance?

TM: Yeah, which card do you have a larger balance?

Me: I've got them both balanced out perfectly. They're the same weight.

TM: And how much do you owe?

Me: Let's see... Zero on one, and zero on the other.

TeleMarketer:

Then go and f___ yourself!

HELLO, SCAMMER

WINDOWS TECH SUPPORT SCAM

WINDOWS TECH SUPPORT SCAM

I have received a small share of the infamous **Windows tech support scam calls**. These scammers attempt to dupe you into giving them access to your computer that allows them to steal your personal information. From there they could clean out your bank account. These people have done tremendous damage, so have no pity upon them. Plus, I don't use a Windows computer...

CALL #1
WINDOWS SUPPORT

LISTEN
CD 2, TRACK 3

WINDOWS**S**CAMMER:

(Thick Indian accent): Thanks for calling Windows support. How can I help you?

Me: Oh hey! Yeah, so someone said that my window was expired?

WS: Yes, your Windows license had expired. You have to renew that.

Me: Oh really? Okay. Um. Which window was it? The one in front, or the one in back, or one of the side ones, or upstairs?

WS: It's your computer Windows license key, sir. It's about your computer.

Me: It's the window next to my computer?

WS: Yes.

Me: Huh. That's weird, cuz I don't have any windows next to my computer.

WS: Sir, it's about your computer, sir, not your home windows. Your Windows license to your operating system, your

Windows 10 license.
Me: Oh, it's the license for the window?
WS: Yes.
Me: Okay. Which window?
WS: Your Windows 10.
Me: I've got... So it's like for 10 windows?
WINDOWSCAMMER:

WINDOWS TECH SUPPORT SCAM
CALL #2
RECRUITING A SCAMMER
TO WORK FOR ME

WINDOWSCAMMER: (with a heavy Indian accent, broken English): Yes, this is Daniel. We are calling you from computer maintenance department of Windows. It's about your computer. How are you doing today?

LISTEN CD 2, TRACK 4

Me: I'm doing really good!
WS: Okay. And I do believe sir are the main user and the owner of your computer?
Me: Yeah, but um... Can I tell you something? Dude! You got a gr...
WS: Let me tell you the reason, sir. The reason I'm calling you is because we are receiving lots of errors and warnings

HELLO, SCAMMER

WINDOWS TECH SUPPORT SCAM

---

          before sending your computer our centralized server. It's indicating that your computer is downloaded some malicious files malfunctionous fiber into your computer without your proper knowledge and without your permission. For past couple of days whenever are you going to online that one of times some hackers are try to access your computer try to misuse your computer...

Me: whoa.

WS: ...without your proper knowledge.

Me: Whoa!

WS: That's the reason we security check the call for you. So can you be in front of your computer at this moment?

Me: WHOA!

WS: And just I show you the problem which is having at your computer and help you about the problem, okay?

Me: Yeah, yeah! It does kinda freak me out a little bit. But dude, I gotta tell you something. What's your name again?

WS: This is Daniel, sir.

Me: Daniel? I gotta tell you something though... Daniel. Dude! You got a *great* speaking voice! Let me tell you something. I run a really similar phone service company here, and man I can tell you, I can use the help. You got a great voice, and I think that you'd be perfect for our company. Is there any way that you would... would you consider coming to work for me?

WS: (surprised/confused): You work... You work to my uh our... You work..?

Me: I wanna hire you! Dude, your voice is fantastic! Your phone voice is fantastic!

WS: Really?

Me: Yeah, yeah! And I wanna hire you.

WS: I will work.

Me: Will you?

HELLO, SCAMMER

WINDOWS TECH SUPPORT SCAM

WS: Yes, I'm work.

Me: Okay, fantastic! That'd be great. I'm so jazzed about this! Whatever they're paying you I'll double it.

WS: How much salary you giving me?

Me: Well, I tell you what. If you send me an email... I betcha they're recording this, right?

WS: Can you tell me how much salary you're giving me?

Me: Whatever they're paying you, I'll double it.

WS: Sorry?

Me: Whatever they're paying you right now, I'll double it.

WS: Oh, okay. Like, uh, can you give me some... like... uh... 200 dollar per month?

Me: 200 dollars per month? Oh yeah. No problem.

WS: Yeah, 200 dollar?

Me: Yeah yeah, no problem. And you can work from home or you can work wherever you want, that's cool. All you need is a phone. Yeah.

WS: Can you tell me your address?

Me: I tell you what. I'll give you my email address, and then send me an email and then what I'll do is I'll respond and we'll work out all the details then. Is that cool?

WS: Okay, can you tell me your email?

Me: Yes. Okay, it's the letter "B" and "S" and the number 867-5309[1].

WS: Yeah?

Me: @BSMail.com

WS: Can you tell me once again? BS-867-5309?

Me: Yes. Uh huh.

WS: Then after that?

Me: @BSMail.com

---

1   Borrowing from Tommy Tutone again.

HELLO, SCAMMER

WINDOWS TECH SUPPORT SCAM

WS: O-kay! @BSMail.com, right?

Me: Yeah.

WS: Okay. Like that is your email address, right?

Me: Yeah, so send me an email and then I'll write back to you and then we'll work out all the details.

WS: Oooo-kay. Um…

Me: I look forward to having you on board. This is exciting.

WS: Can you tell me your address? Like, what country are you live?

Me: We work from anywhere in the world. We're based all over. We got Malaysia and Vietnaaaam and some China call centers. We can use voice talent like you from anywhere in the world.

WS: Sir, where are you living?

Me: Well, you called me here, so you know where I'm living right now! But I'm saying my business is all over the world. So it would be great to have you on board!

WS: But um, sir, um, I am in India.

Me: India? That's fine. Yeah, we work with people in India all the time. Love it.

WS: Do you know Calcutta?

Me: I'm sorry?

WS: Do you know "Cullllcutta"?

Me: Calcutta? Of course. Yeah.

WS: You know Calcutta?

Me: Love it. Yeah. Uh huh.

WS: You love Calcutta?

Me: I love the people, the accents, the voices that come from Calcutta. They're great! It's exactly what we're looking for.

WS: Oh really?

Me: Yeah, exactly.

HELLO, SCAMMER
WINDOWS TECH SUPPORT SCAM

WS: Okay. And so, like, um, how am I going your country? Because I don't have any passport, any visa. So I don't have any much more money.

Me: Well, you have a phone. All you need is a phone.

WS: Yeah, I understand, but how I go in your country?

Me: You don't have to. We'll wire you the money. That's no problem.

WS: You provide money?

Me: Yeah, of course. Yeah, don't worry about it.

WS: Oh really?

Me: Don't worry about it. So send me the email and then I'll reply to you and we'll get this show on the road.

WS: Okay, okay.

Me: Great.

WS: In just a moment, sir, I will send the email, Okay?

Me: Okay. Awesome, Daniel!

WS: Okay. Bye bye.

Me: All right, thank you. All right, bye.

WS: Yeah, bye.

Me: Bye.

WINDOWSSCAMMER:

Hang Up

HELLO, SCAMMER

ROBO-VOICE MEETS MULTI-VOICE

ROBO-VOICE MEETS MULTI-VOICE

LISTEN
CD 2, TRACK 5

Automated telemarketer recording voice:
Oh, the ladies appreciate ya more than you know. What a blessing! So thank you so much for that 50 dollar commitment! And you know what? I'll put my personal stamp on the pledge card just so you remember to tell three women you know and love to schedule a breast cancer screening this year. Now my verifier is gonna click over real quick and make sure that I don't call you back today. Here she is! Please don't hang up!

Different automated telemarketer recording voice (ATM2):
All right then. Just pulling up the screen right now. Give me one second, please...

Hi there, sorry for any delay. This is Jen from verification.

Me: Hi, Jen! [machine can't hear me]

ATM2: And just so you know, this call may be recorded for quality purposes.

Me: Oh really?

ATM2: It says you're going to help with a 50 dollar pledge. Is that correct?

Me: Hey, Jen! What day is it? [testing the machine]

ATM2: Well actually I don't have the answer to that. But if you'd like, I can get my manager and they can answer it for you. It might take 2 or 3 minutes. But would you like me to get him?

Me: Oohhh, yes.

ATM2: Okay, just hold on one second.

(They put me on hold for several minutes.
A live telemarketer comes on.)

HELLO, SCAMMER
ROBO-VOICE MEETS MULTI-VOICE

LiveTeleMarketer:
    (whispered) ha.
Me: ha?
LTM: Hi, Ralph?
Me: Hiiiii.
LTM: Hi, my name is Ron. I'm one of the managers. How can I help you today?
Me: Oh, hi. I don't know. Someone just that uh... that that that that that I wanted to talk to you. I guess. Or you wanted to talk to me? Is that right?
LTM: No problem. Is this 50 dollar donation still Okay?
Me: Oh wait. Is this call being recorded or monitored?
LTM: For quality and control purposes.
Me: Oh, is it? Okay, well. In that case um... hold on. (clears throat) I want to make sure I'm using the best voice possible for the recording...

    (deepening the tone of my voice): How does this sound. Does this sound good?

LTM: Yes.
Me: (deep tone of voice):
Okay, Okay. All right. Because ummmmmMMMMMMMMM....

    (suddenly raising my voice to a high, screechy warble)...

...MMMMMmmmmm... this is mmmmmy urghgghhhhhh mmmmmm REAL VOICE. I've spent mmmmany years working on getting it down to... (voice deepens) down here...

    (voice deepens more to "FM voice")

...to a more sonorous type of sound that's a little more agreeable to most people's ears. And it's something that

HELLO, SCAMMER

ROBO-VOICE MEETS MULTI-VOICE

        I've spent lot of time working on. So do you prefer this voice or the other voice?

LTM: Ummm. It doesn't matter. Either or, whichever is comfortable for...

Me: (high screechy warble):

        MMMMMMmmmmMMMmmmMMMm Okay! Cuz it's actually easier for me to talk in my uuuuuuuuuuurrrrrrrrrrRRRRRRReal voice.

        And ummmmmmmmmmmmmMMMmmMmmmm....

        (switching to disturbing whispery voice):

        I can also do this voice too, because I've worked on this, too—the whisper voice. Cuz like kinda like, you know, it's easier—

LTM: Uhhhh... Sir, thank you so much for your time. You have a great day.

Me: Yeah? MMMMmMMMMMmmMmabout this voice mmmmMmmOkay! Anything else?

LTM: (pause) No, nothing else. You have a great day. Bye bye.

Me: (whisper voice)

        Aaaaaaare you ssssure?

                (no response)

        MMMmmmmmrrrrraaaaaahhHHhhhh... Did I say something wrong?

LIVETELEMARKETER:

CANINE INSURANCE

Automated telemarketer recording voice:
>You are eligible to get THOUSANDS in life insurance benefits! blah blah blah... Press 1 to connect!

Me: (Press 1)

LiveTeleMarketer:
>Hello! Welcome to _____ Insurance. Can I get your name?

Me: Well really, I just want to get my THOUSANDS in life insurance benefits. Can you do that for me?

LTM: Why yes! You can get up to $80,000 in benefits... blah blah blah.

Me: Excellent. I'd like to get my $80,000 for my DOG that died 20 years ago.

LTM: Your dog?

Me: That's right. Can you do that?

LTM: Uh, yeah sure we can do that.

Me: Great. Let's get started!

>(long pause)

LiveTeleMarketer:
>F___ing idiot.

HELLO, SCAMMER

THE BRIAN MATTHEWS SERIES

For a time I got another series of persistent wrong number calls for a "Brian Matthews." Yet another round of debt collectors were after him. Poor guy couldn't catch a break.

But luckily for Brian, he had me to field his calls for him.

TELEPATHY

**LISTEN
CD 2, TRACK 6**

Me: Hello?

Debt Collector:
 Yeah, is Brian Matthews there?

Me: Well, this is Ryan, his twin brother. Can I help you?

DC: Oh, you said you're his twin brother?

Me: Yeah.

DC: Well, I'm calling about a personal business matter for him. Is he available?

Me: Well, we have a telepathic connection, so we've got this special relationship where anything you say to me I relay it to him telepathically, and then back through me. So, I can help you.

DC: (pause...) Okay. Well, I personally was wanting to speak with him. Um.

Me: Well, this is pretty much the same thing. You know telepathy, you know, is kind of like, we put our hands to our temples and concentrate really hard, and I can hear what he's thinking and vice versa. So anything you want me to say, that's cool. I'll telekinetic it over to him. So what would you like me to tell him?

DC: Ahhh, that's fine. I appreciate it. I'll just try back another time.

Me: Well, we can really help you with this. He doesn't like to answer the phone very much, so this is probably the best

HELLO, SCAMMER
THE BRIAN MATTHEWS SERIES

	way to get in touch with him. Actually probably the only way to get in touch with him.
DC:	Is there a better number where I can reach him at?
Me:	No, just this one and the telepath thing. He's got a thing about the phone, ya know? That's why we developed this in childhood and we keep it going now. We have a very unique relationship in that respect. What would you like me to relay to him?
DC:	That's fine. Thank you. Have a nice day.
Me:	Are you sure? Cuz I mean we could get everything figured out. We do business stuff all the time.

DEBT COLLECTOR:

TELEMARKETER NEGOTIATION TIME!

The same folks called back for Brian, but this time tried it with a female telemarketer. Still didn't go very well for them as we negotiated the price of my assistance...

AUTOMATED VOICE:

LISTEN
CD 2, TRACK 7

Press 1 to speak to a live representative. If we have reached the wrong number for <<BRIAN MATTHEWS>> please press 2 to speak to a live representative and we will be happy to remove your phone number. If you are not

HELLO, SCAMMER

THE BRIAN MATTHEWS SERIES

<<BRIAN MATTHEWS>> please hang up or disconnect. By doing...

Don't remember if I pressed 1 or 2. Don't care.

DEBT COLLECTOR:

This is Brittany, how can I direct your call?

Me: Hey, Brittany! Yeah, you guys called me?

DC: *sighs* Let me see, hold on...Ummmm... Yes! Looks like we're trying to reach Brian Matthews.

Me: Yeah? How bad?

DC: Huh?

Me: How bad do you want to reach him?

DC: How <u>bad</u> do I want to reach him?

Me: Yeah.

DC: Is that what you're asking?

Me: Uh huh.

DC: I don't know what you mean by that. Is he available at this number?

Me: Well, that's what I'm asking, is like... Do you <u>really</u> want to reach him? How bad do you want to reach him?

DC: Well, we need to make him aware of some documents we received, so...

Me: So that sounds like, pretty good then?

DC: We have this number up here as a home number to reach him, so that's why we're calling it.

Me: Okay. But I mean, just how bad do you want to talk to him? I mean, I'm just trying to figure out what price...

DC: We need to speak with him! Do you know how we can get in touch with him today?

Me: Well, yeah. **But I charge**. So let's see how much I mean, how much you want to pay.

DC:	Okay, sir. Well you have a great day. I'll call him on another number I have.
Me:	Sooo... you don't want to reach him that bad then?
DC:	No, cuz I'm not gonna go there with you, sir. You have a great day, okay?
Me:	Why did you call then?
DC:	Cuz we have this as his number to reach him.
Me:	Yeah but, we don't give out that information for free. Right?
DC:	(pause) What are you talking about, sir?
Me:	Why did you call? Are you guys in a business?
DC:	(getting louder): CUZ WE HAVE THIS AS!!... (regaining her composure): We have this for Brian Matthews, we have this as his direct number to reach him...
Me:	Okay. And um, did you...
DC:	...as his direct number! I don't understand what you mean by that.
Me:	Yeah so, you're working, right?
DC:	Yes, I am.
Me:	Okay. So the information that I got about Brian is valuable to you, right?
DC:	No, it's not, sir.
Me:	Oh, it's not? Okay.
DC:	It's not that serious.
Me:	It's not that serious? Oh, Okay. Then why did you call?
	(pause)
DC:	I... I'll remove the number, sir. We'll contact him on another number we have for him, okay?
Me:	Well, I hope it gets more serious or less serious depending on the circumstances. Cuz you know... it's nice talking to you, though!
DC:	I don't know where you're trying to get with this call when

HELLO, SCAMMER

THE BRIAN MATTHEWS SERIES

---

	you're… when you're speaking like that! Either this is the wrong number, or this is the right number to reach him. Which… I mean, is it a wrong number..?
Me:	**You gotta pay to find out!**
DC:	I'm…
Me:	You gotta pay to find out.
DC:	I'm not paying anybody to find anything out! I'm sorry.
Me:	Okay!
DC:	I'll get the number removed. Okay?
Me:	Well, whatever you want to do. I mean but, we can negotiate the price if that's the issue.
DC:	(pause) Sir. I don't understand where you're going with this.
Me:	Well, we're making money! Right? You're on the clock, you're making money, right? So am I, so…
DC:	What does that have to do with anything?
Me:	What it has to do with is you want some valuable information and I might have it for you, and so…
DC:	We don't need valuable information, sir…
Me:	It's not?
DC:	…it's not that serious.
Me:	Oh, it's not? Okay. Well then you called though for something not very serious then?
DC:	Yeah, I told you I wanna remove the number so that way we don't call you back and I'll call him on a different number. So I just explained to you.
Me:	Okay, well that's nice.
DC:	All right.
Me:	So, we can drop the price some more if you'd like.
DC:	Sir, I'm wasting my time on this call when I could be

HELLO, SCAMMER
THE BRIAN MATTHEWS SERIES

speaking with Brian, Okay? All right, have a good day.

Me: You sure, even like a 10% discount?

DEBT COLLECTOR:

DEBT COLLECTOR CONFUSION

The bottom-feeding debt collectors persisting in calling for Brian Matthews, so I lovingly made them as impossibly confusing as possible, replete with numerous, doting interruptions...

Me: Okay! Howdy doooo! How are you?

LISTEN
CD 2, TRACK 8

DEBT COLLECTOR:
Is this Brian Matthews?

Me: It's B*w*ian.

DC: All right, Mr. Matthews...

Me: B*w*ian! Yeah who, that, who, yeah, who, who's this?

DC: This is Nathan Morgan...

Me: Nathan!

DC: ...I'm a...

Me: That's yeah! I like that name! Is that "Morgan" like M-O-G-A... with an "E" or an "A"?

DC: M-O-R-G-A-N.

133

HELLO, SCAMMER

THE BRIAN MATTHEWS SERIES

Me: Okay. With another "E" on the end?

DC: No. No "E" on the end.

Me: Okay, cuz that's kinda nice if you put the "E" on the end…

DC: Is…

Me: …it's kind of little bit of a French sort of thing to it. Um. Yeah. So Nathan! Yeah. Are you having a good day?

DC: I am, um, I'm…

Me: Yeah??

DC: …calling…

Me: What?

DC: …from one main.

Me: From who?

DC: I'm calling from one main.

Me: One main?

DC: Yes.

Me: Is that your street address?

DC: I'm sorry?

Me: Is that your street address?

DC: No. One main is the name of the company.

Me: Oh, Okay. So you guys do like, pave main streets then?

DC: No, sir…

Me: Ooooh.

DC: …we're a loan company.

Me: What? It's a loan? Why would you call it "one main" then? It sounds like you're a street company.

DC: Yeeeeeaah…

Me: Ummm….

DC: …I need to…

Me: Have you thought about changing your name?

DC: This is…

134

HELLO, SCAMMER
THE BRIAN MATTHEWS SERIES

Me: I mean...

DC: ...this is Brian Matthews, correct?

Me: ...This is, well, it's B<u>w</u>ian. Yeah, and this is Nathan?

DC: Yes, let me...

Me: Yeah. Uh huh.

DC: ...let me first to...

Me: So?

DC: ...ensure the quality of service that we provide, this call may be...

Me: What?

DC: ...monitored or recorded.

Me: Oh, it is?! Who's monitoring and recording it?

DC: It's systematically done, it's...

Me: Yeah? What's the name of the system, that's recording it? I just wanna say...

DC: Elvia.

Me: It's Elvia? That's a nice name for a system. Hey, Elvia!! Can I talk to it?

DC: I mean, it's recording our whole conversation, so...

Me: Oh, is it? Okay. Can I record? I got an Elvira, too. Can I record over here? Too?

DC: You can.

Me: What's that? Yeah, cuz then the two of ours can talk to each other. At some point.

DC: All right.

Me: Yeah.

DC: I have to first say...

Me: So.

DC: ...to ensure the quality of the service we provide this call may be monitored or recorded, Mr. Matthews.

HELLO, SCAMMER
THE BRIAN MATTHEWS SERIES

Me: Well.. I don't really want to ensure the quality. Can we, like, you know…. That doesn't really matter to me that much. So can we do away with the quality part?

DC: All right. Also, this is an attempt to collect a debt by a debt collector, and…

Me: And this is..? I thought you were a paving company.

DC: …for that purpose.

Me: I thought you were a paving company?

(talking over each other)

DC: No sir, I…

Me Oh!

DC: …informed you that we…

Me: This is..?

DC: …I mean we are a…

Me: Oooooh! That's right…

DC: …also…

Me: …you do loans AND paving! At the same time! How do you guys do all that stuff?!

DC: You currently have a balance…

Me: It's..?

DC: …of 1,130 dollars and 43 cents…

Me: Oh.

DC: …can you pay this today?

Me: Wait, so you guys owe me one thousand how much?

For the paving?

Cuz you know we paved one street and then we sent a bill for that. We still haven't been paid. Is that what you're talking about?

(pause)

136

HELLO, SCAMMER
THE BRIAN MATTHEWS SERIES

DC: Just one second.
Me: Well hold on! I mean...

(DC puts me on hold)

Me: One-one thousand. Okay. Two Mississippi. Threeeeeeee.... Hey Nathan? Hey.
DC: I'm here, sir...
Me   Yeah?
DC: ...Mr. Matthews?
Me: Yeah, that was more than a second. I counted it. I did like... "One-one thousand," then "two-Mississippi," and I even just said, "Threeeeeee...." And, you didn't come back.
DC: (silence)
Me: Hello?
DC: Yes...
Me: Yeah?
DC: ...Mr. Matthews?
Me: Uh. Yeah Nathan? What's up?
DC: Yeah.. I'm calling about your one main personal loan that you have with us. We were trying to assist you in getting it back current. I got...
Me: Oh?
TM   ...you currently have a balance due...
Me: That's...
DC: ...on this loan...
Me: ...great!
DC: ...of 1,130 dollars and 43 cents.
Me: Yeah?
DC: Can you pay this today?
Me: Well, I'm wondering if you can pay me for the paving that we did? Can we get that all taken care of?

HELLO, SCAMMER

THE BRIAN MATTHEWS SERIES

DC: (silence)

Me: Um, hello?

DC: Yeah, I'm here.

Me: Yeah, I mean I though that's what you're calling about over on Main Street. And then the other time we strung the lights up over the top of that? Are they still up? Or did you guys take them down?

(pause)

DC: Okay, I wouldn't know what you're speaking of, sir…

Me: Ooh, well I thought…

TM   …I'm talking about your one main…

Me: …I thought we knew each other. I thought you knew what we're talking about. So um…

    Yeah. Okay so…yeah. Do you want me to count to "one-Mississippi, two" again? So you can think about it..?

DC: No! We're calling about your loan, sir!

Me: Yeah, who..?

DC: Your monthly payment is 170 dollars and 3 cents a month…

Me: So "we" – so it's like you and…

DC: …on your account…

Me: So it's..?

DC: …can you make any type of payment on the account today?

Me: Yeah but, who's "we"? Is that you and Elvira? Computer?

(long pause)

DC: Mmmkay, sir. I'm calling about your, your personal loan account.

Me: Your personal loan account?

DC: Can you make a payment on your account or no?

Me: Well, I'm just wondering if, about the lights that are… up. So…

HELLO, SCAMMER

THE BRIAN MATTHEWS SERIES

DC: All right, have a good…

Me: …and then…

DC: …day, sir.

Me: Well hold on! We're just trying to figure out what's going on! Um…

DC: (silence)

Me: Hello?

DC: (silence)

Me: One-one thousand, two-Mississippi…

Debt Collector:

BRIAN THE DOG

Who says the callee has to be human?

Debt Collector:
Yes, sir. I'm looking for Brian.

Me: Looking for Brian? Okay.

DC: Yes.

Me: Let's see if we can find him.

DC: Thank you.

Me: (sounds of walking around the house, doors opening and closing, etc.)

You know, he hides sometimes, because he's afraid of the phone.

LISTEN
CD 2, TRACK 9

HELLO, SCAMMER
THE BRIAN MATTHEWS SERIES

DC: Ooo-kay.

Me: So I'm checking every noook and cranny. Let's see if I can find Brian.

(raising voice as if calling to an animal): Brian! (cheerful whistling)

Let's see…. Oh, there you are! Good boy. Good boy!

(talking back to the telemarketer):

Okay, so what do you want with Brian?

DC: Um, is this Brian Matthews?

Me: **Brian is a dog.**

DC: (pause) Oh, Brian is a dog?

Me: Yeah. Do you still want to talk to Brian?

DC: No, I'm looking for Brian Matthews. Is he available?

Me: Yeah, that's the dog.

DC: Ooooo-kay. All right.

(smugly): When's a good time I can reach Mr. Brian Matthews?

Me: What's that?

DC: When's a good time I can reach Mr. Brian Matthews?

Me: He's right here!

DC: Ooo-kay.

Me: So who is this? Is there another dog that wants to talk to him?

DC: (pause) No, I'm just looking for Brian Matthews.

Me: Well you got him, right here! He's wagging his tail.

(longer pause)

DC: All right. Well sir, um, I'll… what's a good number for me to reach the real Brian Matthews?

Me: I just told you! You got him right here! So you don't want to talk to…? Well I mean, I might be able to get him to bark.

HELLO, SCAMMER
THE BRIAN MATTHEWS SERIES

(pause)

DC: Okay, um...

Me: Who is this?

DC: ...one second, cuz I'm actually trying... My name is _____.

Me: Hey, _____! Yeah. What's your last name?

DC: Um, my name is _____ Ferguson sir.

Me: "Fergusonsir"?

DC: Yes, sir.

Me: So it's "Fergusonsir." All right. So... I'm not quite sure why you want to talk to the dog.

DC: Umm..

Me: But we've got stranger calls than that!

DC: Right.

Me: Yeah?

DC: Um, so... This is not a good number for Brian, sir? Other than for a...

Me: For "Briansir"?

DC: ...a dog?

Me: I mean, the dog is here.

DC: Mmm-huh.

Me: (to the "dog"): Brian!! No no! No chewing on the table! No. All right. Bad boy.

DC: All right. Well sir, thank you so much for taking the call. You have a wonderful day. Mmm-huh, bye bye.

Me: I enjoyed this.

DEBT COLLECTOR:

HELLO, SCAMMER

THE BRIAN MATTHEWS SERIES

GETTIN' TESTY WITH THE TELEMARKETER

Here is another prime example of the kind of folks often at the other end of debt collector calls: downright ornery people. Once you get beyond the pleasantries and they don't get what they want—your money and/or private information—all cordialities are off. This is why we have no sympathy messing with them...

LISTEN
CD 2, TRACK 10

DEBT COLLECTOR:
    I'm trying to reach Brian.
Me: Brian? Hmmm.
DC: Correct.
Me: How much is that worth to you?
DC: To me, I mean... It's a little hard work. I could find him, but... He must have a situation with you, too.
Me: Well now, if you're looking for him, probably you're making some money off this, right? If you find him, right?
DC: Well, no. This is regarding a legal matter.
Me: Ohhh, Okay. So yeah, so you do make some money off of it then.
DC: Ehhhh, I mean, it depends on the situation. Depends on how far we have to actually go ahead and try to pursue him.
Me: Okay. Well, I tell you what. Whatever money you make, we'll split it.
DC: *laughs* We'll split it?
Me: Yeah!
DC: Uhhhh...
Me: Obviously finding him, that's some valuable information, isn't it?
DC: Not at all.

HELLO, SCAMMER
THE BRIAN MATTHEWS SERIES

Me: It's not?

DC: In this situation, not at all.

Me: Oh, it's not. Okay.

DC: If it comes to litigation, if they go ahead and can't establish communication with the avenues that he's provided, we just basically release the documentation there.

Me: Okay, so you're <u>not</u> getting paid?

DC: I'm trying to figure out, what is the intention at this point?

Me: Well, to split it! Obviously this is valuable information to you.

DC: Not that valuable....

Me: It's not that valuable to you? Oh, Okay.

DC: ...It's not something that we can't obtain on our own.

Me: So you just called to chat about the weather?

DC: No, your actual information was placed on a file. That's why we're trying to find him.

Me: So? Still, you're not working for free, are you?

DC: (pause)

Me: Are you?

DC: What is your question??

Me: Split it. Pay me. Right?

DC: Are you in need of a job?

Me: I'm in need of whatever you're making. I get a piece of it if I help you out.

DC: That's not gonna happen.

Me: Well then why should I help you?

DC: I really don't care if you do! Like I said...

Me: Then why did you call?

DC: ...if you can get Brian...

Me: Then why did you call?

143

HELLO, SCAMMER

THE BRIAN MATTHEWS SERIES

(Now he starts getting mad.)

DC: If you would stop talking and listen you could actually learn something…

Me: Oh..?

DC: …but you're still talking and not listening!

Me: Okay yeah, you called me.

DC: Again, this is why you're not learning!

Me: I'm not interested in learning; I'm interested in making some money.

DC: …and I'll go ahead and establish communication. If he doesn't, we'll release the appearance. If he doesn't appear on that, man, you gotta hire a lawyer! I really don't care if Brian shows up or not. But if you want to play games, I have **nothing but time**. I get paid for this! Do you?

(So now we've established that he's making money. Good.)

Me: Yes. So how much are you gonna pay me to help you?

(He tries switching to mockery)

DC: So like I said, you must be a bored person.
If you want to transcribe the message to him, not a problem. If not, go about your day. Go find some money!

Me: Okay, how much are you gonna pay me now?

DC: Again! Like I said! Do you understand what I just said to you??

Me: Nope.

DC: It's not that hard. Based on English is the dialect we all understand. I said, if you don't understand what I'm saying to you, if you don't want to take the messages it's no skin off my back. You're not helping Brian. I really don't care what you do.

Me: So how's the weather where you are?

DC: It's absolutely beautiful.

Me: Okay, that's lovely.

HELLO, SCAMMER
THE BRIAN MATTHEWS SERIES

DC: Any other questions at this point?
Me: Yeah, yeah. What else are you doing?
DC: Listen!
Me: So what else are you doing?
DC: Listen! I'm not gonna waste time with you!
Me: But you just said you have all the time in the world. So what are you doing?
DC: It's 12:48! Unfortunately, if you don't have a job that's on you.
Me: Yeah, so what else are you doing?
DC: I mean...
Me: Do you play croquet?
DC: ...other than that...
Me: Do you croquet?
DC: Do you understand, you're not gonna dictate this conversation!
Me: Do you play...?
DC: It's not worth that much! So if you...
Me: ...croquet?
DC: ...have any other questions, because Brian...
Me: Do you do...?
DC: ...is not worth being an idiot and actually trying to get him litigated at this point!
Me: What else do you do for hobbies?
DC: Do you understand simple English or not?
Me: What else do you do for hobbies?
DC: DO YOU UNDERSTAND SIMPLE ENGLISH OR NOT, SIR?
Me: Do you like to play...
       (totally talking over each other now)
DC: You grab the paper, you find you a job!...

HELLO, SCAMMER

THE BRIAN MATTHEWS SERIES

Me: ...Do you like...

DC: ...you do your job. I don't like you doing mine! Okay?

Me: ...Do you like to do..?

DC: ...We're not gonna go ahead and play these games. I don't do this with...

Me: Do you like chocolate?

DC: ...individuals I know and I'm not gonna do it with somebody that's a stranger.

Me: Do you like chocolate?

DC: Sad! Sad that a man...

Me: Do you like Bonbons?

DC: ...that's sad!

Me: Do you like sugar-covered Bonbons?

DC: I don't like anything sugary! I can see you do...

Me: Oh Okay. Do you like, um...

DC: ...all right, buddy!...

Me: Are you a vegetarian then?

DC: ...I hope you can find something to do, though! Because a grown man not having any...

Me: Are you...?

DC: ...is really sad!!

Me: So you're calling people and you're calling ME sad? That's pretty funny.

DC: No yeah, but see I get paid and you don't!!

Me: Oh, oh. Right! See, you do get paid for it! Ahhh..!

DC: (mimicking me) Ahhhhhh!

Me: So now...

DC: I'm just saying...

Me: ...how much of the piece you're getting are you gonna pay me?

146

HELLO, SCAMMER
THE BRIAN MATTHEWS SERIES

DC: Are you that hard up for money?

Me: My time is valuable, too.

DC: A grown man should be able to make his own way!

Me: Awwww... You don't even know what I do, do you?

DC: (mumbling) It doesn't matter.

Me: Okay, so do you ummm...

DC: I don't!... (stammering on unintelligibly)

Me: What kind of light bulbs do you have in your house?

DC: ...I'll let them know that you... you're... y-you're... (*uncomfortably laughs *) I'll let them know what's going on.

Me: What kind of light bulbs do you have?

DC: And I'll make sure they get Brian's information out, Okay? I really do hope you find some sort of employment. It's sad.

Me: And what else are you doing now?

DC: *grumbles*

Me: What else are you doing?

DC: Okay, buddy. You have a good day, all right? I hope you find something to do.

Me: Like you?

DC: All right. You have a good day, buddy.

Me: What's your name? Hello?

DEBT COLLECTOR:

MUSICAL CALLS

HELLO, SCAMMER

LET'S SING!

TeleMarketer:
(heavy Indian accent): I'm saying that I'm calling you from lower your insurance rates dot com. I do believe you still paying for your car insurance?

Me: (cheery low voice): Oh, Yah. Oooh, yah!

TM: So if we beat your rates and offer you a lot lot, and a lot cheaper rates, with the same amount of coverage you have, would you at least think about it after comparison?

LISTEN
CD 2, TRACK 11

Me: Ohh yah.

TM: Okay, so can you please tell me, your last name is Jones, it's J-O-N-E-S, right?

Me: Ooh, right. Right.

TM: And your first name is spelled like that J-O-H-N, right?

Me: Oh yeah. Right. Right.

TM: Yes sir! Sure. I'm saying is that we will get our rate specialist to call you to discuss your personalized savings.

Me: Uayah.

TM: Do we have your permission to call you back?

Me: If you sing. I have a song that I sing. Can you sing with me?

TM: What's that?

Me: Sing the song with me first.

TM: Sir, I just uh... I... I don't...

Me:

Allegro

Hum di-dil-y hum di-dil-y hum di-dil-y hum di-dil-y HUM!

HELLO, SCAMMER

MUSICAL CALLS

Me: Can you do that?
TM: No, sir. I don't…

Allegro

Hum di-dil-y hum di-dil-y hum di-dil-y hum di-dil-y   HUM!

TM: Ooooooohhhhh I… I, I don't have any time…
Me: Try it!
TM: …for…
Me: Tryyyyy it! Come on!

Allegro

Hum di-dil-y hum di-dil-y hum di-dil-y hum di-dil-y   HUM!

TM: (pause) Well I don't, I don't understand what I'm saying.
Me: We have to do this to proceed on. It's just what I do. Just go with me! Come on!!

Allegro

Hum di-dil-y hum di-dil-y hum di-dil-y hum di-dil-y   HUM!

TM: Have a great day.
Me: TRY IT!
TM: I…
Me: TRY IT!!!

HELLO, SCAMMER

MUSICAL CALLS

TeleMarketer:

MUNCHA BUNCHA CRUNCHA HOTLINE

TELEMARKETER:
 Hello?
Me: (singing)...

♪ Munch a bunch a munch a crunch-a! Munch a bunch a munch a crunch-a! ♪

TM: (singing back) ♫♪ Da da da da da da da da, Da da da da da da da... ♫♪
Me: Aw yeah! Everybody together now...

♪ Munch a bunch a munch a crunch-a! Munch a bunch a munch a crunch-a! ♪

TM: Come on, sing it again!
Me: Thank you for calling the Hemorrhoid Hotline. Press (1) for suppositories. Press (2) for ointment.
TM: What happens if I press 4?
Me: I'm sorry, that's not a valid entry. Please try again.
TM: What about 5?
Me: It sounds like you're having trouble. Would you like to speak to an operator?

HELLO, SCAMMER

MUSICAL CALLS

TM: Yes.
Me: Operator, may I help you?
TM: Yeah, do the song again!
Me: I'm sorry, that's paid function.
TM: How much?
Me: $500.
TM: Okay, give me your account number and we'll send it to you.
Me: I'm sorry, we only accept cash.
TM: Okay, then do the song again, then we'll send it to you.
Me: I'm sorry, payment must be made in advance.
TM: Come on!
Me: It sounds like you're having trouble...
TELEMARKETER:
   Okay, hang up then.

HELLO, SCAMMER

MEDICARE CALLS

MEDICARE SCAMMERS

These scammers called for "Peggy," so of course I obliged and became "Peggy" for them. Pretty sure they appreciated that…

Me: [in a high, feminine voice]: Hello?

LISTEN
CD 2, TRACK 12

Medicare Scammer 1: Hello, Mrs. Peggy?

Me: Yes?

MS1: Good morning.

Me: Good morningggg!

MS1: It's Gene with _____ home of special rate insurance on a recorded line.

Me: Yeah? Hi!!

MS1: Mrs. Stanfeld, you may be eligible for Medicare plan that adds up to 1,200 dollars back to your social security check in buy-back benefits per year.

Me: That sounds wonderful!

MS1: Will get you to a licensed insurance agent to check if you're eligible. And Mrs. Peggy, in order to connect you with the correct licensed Medicare agent, can you please confirm the state you live in? Are you still in _____?

Me: Yeah, sometimes. Yeah, I think so.

MS1: All right. Okay.

Me: What state are you in?

MS1: Yeah, actually I'm asking your state because _____ has different guidelines and need a

HELLO, SCAMMER

MEDICARE CALLS

	specific licensed agent. And I need to make sure I connect you with a licensed agent in your state. Okay?
Me:	Yeah yeah, but I'm wondering what's your state, too? Cuz I'm wondering, just maybe we know each other? Maybe we're neighbors?
MS1:	Oh um, hello?
Me:	Yes?
MS1:	Actually I'm calling from California.
Me:	Oooh, Okay. We're probably not neighbors then. Probably not.
MS1:	[trying to get back on script]:
	Okay. So let me now, Mrs. Peggy, let me now connect you to our licensed Medicare agent in your state to give you a free plan check. This will be quick, Okay?
Me:	Okay, will he be neighbors, too?
MS1:	Um, let's see. You can talk to our licensed Medicare agent.
Me:	Okay.
MS1:	Stay on the line!
Me:	When I'm in California can I come say hi to you..?
MS1:	[cuts me off, putting me on hold. After a brief hold, comes back on]:
	And now, Mrs. Peggy, we are waiting for a licensed agent on the line and I will introduce you on page on the call, Okay?
Me:	Okay!

HELLO, SCAMMER

MEDICARE CALLS

Medicare Scammer 2 now joins the call.

> MS2: Thank you for calling _____, home of the special rate insurance, helping health conscious people with special rates.
>
> MS1: Here you go, Peggy, your agent just joined the line and he will take great care of you from here. Have a wonderful day.
>
> **Me**: Hi!!!
>
> MS2: Thank you.
> [super cheery voice]: Hi, Peggy!
>
> **Me**: Hi!!!!
>
> MS2: Hi there. Okay, my name is _____ Mines. And I'm licensed insurance agent.
>
> **Me**: Like "mines"? Like landmines?
>
> MS2: [laughs] Yeah, landmines, or goldmines, or…
>
> **Me**: Yeah. That's a funny name!
>
> MS2: [perplexed pause]
> Thank you.
>
> **Me**: Yeah?
>
> MS2: Uh. Okay. And I am a licensed insurance agent in the state of _____ on a recorded line here.
>
> **Me**: Yeah? How do I see the license? Can I see the license?
>
> MS2: Sure! You can look it up on the state of _____ department of insurance website there.
>
> **Me**: Yeah? But can you like, make me a copy?
>
> MS2: Well you can pull it up from there.

HELLO, SCAMMER

MEDICARE CALLS

Me: Yeah but can you make me a... I wanna make sure like, like a color copy of it. Can you?

MS2: Sure. You can pull it up from there and print it out. Yes.

Me: Can you mail me a copy?

MS2: [*sighs*]
Are you want to be serious about this or are you just messing around here?

Me: No! I told them I'm serious about this.

MS2: Okay then! Would you like to discuss your Medicare options here?

Me: Yeah, but that makes me sad that you don't think I'm serious.

MS2: Okay well, again, you can go to the department of insurance and pull up my license there. I can give you my license number.

Me: Okay.

MS2: Would you like that?

Me: Yeah yeah!

MS2: Okay.

Me: Okay, go.

MS2: Get a piece of paper and let me know when you're ready.

Me: Okay, hold on. Okay, start! Okay, go ahead!

MS2: It's 1 7

Me: Yeah.

MS2: 1 2 8 [pauses] 7 _____

Me: Okay.

155

HELLO, SCAMMER

MEDICARE CALLS

Well, shoot! My pen just ran out of ink. Hang on.

[pause]

You know how pens run out of ink?

MS2: Right.

Me: Yeah, yeah. It's like that.
Um, darnit. Okay, I think this one... I *think* this one works.

[banging a pen sound in background]

I *think*... Yeah, Okay give it to me again.

MS2: [getting exasperated]:

1 7

Me: Yeah?

MS2: 1 2 8...

Me: Oh wait, it just ran... Dangit. It just ran out again!

Hold on.

[pause]

Now I'm looking for paper.

[pause]

Darnnaggit. How come there's never a piece of paper around when you need one?

Medicare Scammer 2:

HELLO, SCAMMER

MEDICARE CALLS

🖐 POSTSCRIPT

I later checked for this scammer's purported license number on the state department of insurance website. It did not exist. A search for anyone licensed under the name he gave me also didn't exist. Beware.

TESSI'S NOT TESTY

Medicare Scammer:
Hello, is this Peggy?

LISTEN
CD 2, TRACK 13

Me: (phony feminine voice): Hi!

MS: Ahh, is this Peggy Seinview?

Me: Yup, uh-huh! Sure is! How are you? What's your name?

MS: My name is Tessi and I'm calling from the Medicare Help Center. How are you today?

Me: I'm lovely. It's so nice to hear from you!

MS: Okaaaay. The reason for my call, Peggy, is to do a policy overview on Medicare beneficiaries to see if they qualify for the new upgrade. And just to be sure, Peggy, you have Medicare parts A and B?

Me: Yeah, your name is Tessi?

MS: Yes.

Me: Okay. It sounds like "testy" but it's not. You don't sound very testy.

MS: Okaaay.

Me: You sound really nice!

MS: (sound of other Medicare scammers in the background)

HELLO, SCAMMER

MEDICARE CALLS

Me: Have you thought about changing your name slightly just to make sure there's no mix-ups? I don't want anybody to think you're testy.

MS: My name is Tessi. T-E-S-S-I.

Me: Yeah, I know. But it's really close to "testy," and I would really hate for people to get you mixed up and think it's "testy."

MS: Okay, I see.

Me: And you know the other thing that "testis" means, right? You know, like cough and (*cough cough*) and turn your head?

MS: Okaaay..

Me: Yeah, you don't want to get confused! Maybe... you could have like "Tessa." Maybe? That would be a little better.

MS: (laughs) Okaaay.. Ahh... (unintelligible)

Me: How about...? Oh, I know! "Tesla!" It's so popular right now!

MS: Okaaay..

Me: Elon would <u>love</u> you!

MS: Ahh, do you have Medicare parts A & B?

Me: I think so. Yeah, yeah. Every time I hear you talk, I just want to say "testy" and I gotta smack myself over and over over over... (smacking forehead over and over)... and say, nope nope nope nope, it's <u>Tessa</u>! Or is it "Tesla"? See, I'm all confused now!

MS: Okaaay.. Let me ask, what Medicare benefits do you use the most?

Me: Testy.
I mean... nope! (exasperated gasp) You see what I mean? Dangnabit!

HELLO, SCAMMER
MEDICARE CALLS

MS: (pauses) Would you like a call back?

Me: No! Nope, nope, everything is good. Everything's good.

MS: Okay, would you like the Medicare upgrade?

Me: Yeah. You're not getting testy though, are you?

MS: No, I'm not.

Me: Okay, good. Because we don't *want that*!

MS: (pauses) I'm not.

Me: Okay, good.

MS: Okay?

Me: Okay. Good, good. Just, just keep reassuring me that everything's Okay.

MS: Okay. Peggy you have...

Me: Where are you calling from?

MS: I'm calling from the Medicare Help Center.

Me: I know. Where is that located?

MS: In Miami, Florida.

Me: I *love* Miami!

MS: Oh wow, you do?

Me: Yeaaaah. You guys have great, great cigars down there. Gives me a cough though.

MS: Sorry about that.

Me: Can you hear it in my voice?

MS: Yes, I do.

Me: Yeah! (hacking coughs) I get testy sometimes when I think about cigars. It's all

HELLO, SCAMMER

MEDICARE CALLS

---

	your fault! You know what I'm saying? I'm just kidding!
MS:	Okay, well you have a good day, Okay Peggy?
Me:	Okay, testy. I mean..! (exasperated gasp) Jeez, I keep doing it over over over over again! (smacking forehead over and over again)
MS:	Why?
Me:	Because it's your name is mixing me up!
MS:	(groans) Okay, bye.
Me:	I wanna talk some more about this!
MS:	I'll call you back, Okay?
Me:	(meekly): You're not gonna be testy when you call back, are you?
MS:	No, I'm not.
Me:	Okay. 'Cuz that would make me really... I would be really disappointed. You sound so nice!
MS:	Thank you!
Me:	(gushy): Yeaaah.
MS:	(pause) Okay, have a good day.
Me:	Yeah, but...
MS:	Bye!
Me:	...it makes me sad that you're going away. Don't.
MS:	(trying not to laugh)
Me:	(whimpering): don't.
MS:	(trying to compose herself): Could you give me a minute?
Me:	(desperately): Okay.

HELLO, SCAMMER

MEDICARE CALLS

                    (pause)

MS: Hello?

Me: Hello!? Hi!

MS: Yes, hi.

Me: Tesla! Hi, Tesla.

MS: Are you interested in the Medicare benefits?

Me: Yeah, Tessi, yeah I sure am. But I just got a cigar, my last one from Miami, and I'm just gonna light it up here in just a second.

MS: (silence, trying to understand what's going on): Okaaay... Um, so... What Medicare benefits do you use the most?

Me: You know, I'm just thinking about cigars at the moment. Hang on. Just a second.

MS: (trying not to laugh): Would you like a call back?

Me: No, but you got me thinking cigars! And you got me thinking Cubans now, too! Dangnabit. Tessi!

MS: (gasps and whimpers)

Sometimes the goal is to get them to say ridiculous things...

HELLO, SCAMMER

"SIMON SAYS" CALLS

PUMPKINHEAD LARRY

TeleMarketer:
Hello, I'm Ann _____ in the verification department, and I'll be making sure everything is correct. How are you doing today?

Me: (In a very nervous, wavering voice):
Hi. I'm I'm... um. Pretty good. How are you?

TM: I'm good, thank you for asking. And how much did you promise to donate?

Me: Ummmmm, I think it was the... middle amount?

LISTEN
CD 2, TRACK 14

TM: It was the what, I'm sorry?

Me: The middle amount.

TM: Well, I can put in the computer anything between 15 and 99.

Me: Ooooooooo boy. Um. (*gasping*) Whew. Um...

TM: The 15 dollars is the lowest.

Me: Yeah, ummm... Hey, this call is really suddenly making me really nervous.
(*taking deep breath – exhale....*)
Can you say something to calm me down a little bit?

TM: Well sir, I do apologize about your, you know, probably your anxiety. I can just get you out information, that way you're not *promising* anything. In that way you can look it over and make sure you're comfortable with your decision.

Me: Well, actually your voice is kinda soothing. It's... it's feeling a little better now.

TM: Thank you.

Me: Yeah.

TM: That was very sweet. Thank you.

162

HELLO, SCAMMER
"SIMON SAYS" CALLS

Me: Okay, thanks. Yeah.
Um, Okay. Where were we? Again?

TM: Well, would you like me to send you out some information? That way you're not promising any commitment. Then you can look it over.

Me: No, that's fine. We can proceed on.

TM: (cheerfully): Okay! Well, how much would you want to donate?

Me: Ummm, what were the...

TM: An amount that you're comfortable with.

Me: ...what were the choices again?

TM: Well, I can put anything between 15 dollars one time, and 99.

Me: Okay. Um... I'm thinking toward the higher end, but (getting super nervous again)...

OoooOooohoooOho, man... Whooooooo! (*gasping*) I just got anther wave of anxiety just thinking about it!

Can you say hey, "**Settle down Pumpkinhead?**" Just say that!

TM: How about you **settle down, Pumpkinhead**.

Me: Okay... (breathing slower)

TM: Is that it?

Me: All right. Say that again!

TM: Now, do you have a name?

Me: Yeah. I mean you can call me Lar.... Larry.

Say the Pumpkinhead thing again! That makes me feel better.

TM: Okay, I'll say it, but what is your name?

Me: Larry.

TM: Larry?

Me: Say, "Settle down..."

TM: **Pumpkinhead!**

HELLO, SCAMMER

"SIMON SAYS" CALLS

Me: "...Pumpkinhead Larry!"

TM: (sweetly): **Larry Pumpkinhead**.

Me: (meekly): thank you.

TM: **Pumpkinhead Larry**. How about that?

Me: Thank you. Yeah...

(** deep breath **)

Okay.

TM: That's it. So let me put you down for maybe a minimum of 10 or 15 dollars?

Me: Ummmmm....

Y-y-yeah, yeah. I think, yeah. That feels a little bit better. I'd like to do more, but I just feel this wave of anxiety come over me when...

TM: I understand. I have the same problem.

Me: You do?

TM: I do have anxiety. Yes, sir.

Me: You do? Okay. Does the **Pumpkinhead** thing work for you, too?

TM: No.

Me: It doesn't? Okay.

TM: My son. I picture my son's little smile, and it helps me!

Me: Okay.

TM: Yes, it helps.

Me: I get that. Okay.

TM: Yeah, that works.

Me: **Pumpkinhead** works with me.

TM: Now **Pumpkinhead**, what is your last name?

Me: Oooh, boy. It's coming back again!...

(*starts hyperventilating*)

(*deep breathing in and out directly into the phone*)

BbbbbbrrbrrRRBbrbbrBRRRBRRBrrrbRBR!!!

HELLO, SCAMMER

"SIMON SAYS" CALLS

OoooOooohooOoooHooooooo...

(*slower breathing*)

Okay. All Right um...

TeleMarketer:
Thank you. Bye bye.

HELLO, SCAMMER

"SIMON SAYS" CALLS

INTERNET COLORS

LISTEN
CD 2, TRACK 15

This telemarketer was treated to the best lethargic, unenthusiastic voice I could doldrum out. Not sure if he appreciated it.

Me: (like I'm just waking up): Yeah Okay? What are you calling about?

TeleMarketer:
We're calling about our fiber optic Internet with a permanent discount. We now have Internet speeds up to 1,000 megabits per second. So we're just wondering if that may be something you're interested in today, sir?

Me: What... what colors does it come in?

TM: I'm sorry?

Me: What colors do the fiber come in? Is it blue or tan? I like... I like tan.

TM: I.....'m not sure, sir.

Me: Can you check with someone about that?

TM: You mean like what color is the cabling?

Me: You know, what color does the fiber come in? Is it... Ya know? I'm Okay with blue. And tan. Tan is kinda nice, too. Um. But I want to make sure that the color is the right one first. So, can you check on that first for me?

TM: Okay. And do you mean by the color of the cabling, or the..?

Me: The color of the service.

TM: You can't see the serv... the color of the fiber optic, like, line on the inside.

Me: Well, that's important to me, though. I want to know what

HELLO, SCAMMER
"SIMON SAYS" CALLS

	color everything is. You know, cuz we're real sensitive about that around here. Um, because we've taken a lot of...
TM:	Oooooh, Okay.
Me:	...we've taken a lot of time to get the color scheme just right, and we want to make sure the internet is also the right color. So. You know?
TM:	You are currently on our service already. It would just be an upgrade from what you have now. So still the same wire that's coming into your home, just faster.
Me:	Oh, we are? Okay then.
TM:	You're on our megabit per second service.
Me:	When it gets faster, does it get like uh... Does it get hotter? Too?
TM:	No, sir.
Me:	It doesn't? Okay. Because. You know. If it got hotter that would change the color. Probably. You know, it starts to **glow**? Kind of.
TM:	Yeeeah. No, sir.
Me:	It doesn't glow?
TM:	It...
Me:	Cuz we actually would like that. We'd like that! Could we get the glowing... kind?
TM:	...what you have but faster.
Me:	Can I get the glowing kind?
TM:	No, sir.
Me:	We can't? Oh. I don't know if we're interested if it doesn't... glow.
TM:	All right, sir. Not a problem.
Me:	But, do you... would you..?
TM:	If you ever decide if you want to upgrade faster, you just let us know.

HELLO, SCAMMER

"SIMON SAYS" CALLS

Me: Well, it's the color's the thing that's really what we're concerned about here.

TM: Yeah, well as I said, sir, there's no color to the service. It would just make your service faster for you.

Me: Does the... uh... are there... does it come with, like... are pets good with it, too?

TM: Well, are your pets fine with the service now?

Me: No, we're hoping pets come with the service.

TM: Ooooh, you want pets to come with the service?

Me: Yeeeeah.

TM: Ahh, Okay. Unfortunately, no. It would just be a new modem router. Basically make your service faster. It's the only reason why I'm calling today is to help you make your services faster and better for you and just let you know about it.

Me: Oh. Okay. Is... What about in the shower? Can, you know... can we put it in the shower? Too?

TM: I don't think so, sir.

Me: What about the washing machine? Can we, um... put the faster speed in the washing machine? Will it make the washer go faster?

TM: I don't think so, sir.

Me: Wellll-Okay. Ummmm... How does it affect the weather over our house? Does it..?

TM: It would probably tell you how the weather works and faster for you.

Me: It would..?

TM: It would get it there faster for you, tell you what the weather's gonna be.

Me: No. I'm wondering like how it changes the weather over the house. Does it make it sunnier?

TM: No!

HELLO, SCAMMER

"SIMON SAYS" CALLS

Me: It doesn't make it sunnier, or..?

TM: No, I don't believe so, sir.

Me: It doesn't? Okay, well...

TM: Anyway sir, if this isn't something you're interested in I'm going to have to disconnect the call, Okay?

Me: No, we're interested! I'm just wondering like... how...?

TM: Fifty dollars per month plus your state sales tax for the services...

Me: Does it kill..?

TM: ...no costs, no activation fee. Is that something you'd be interested in today?

Me: Does it kill the weeds in the yard?

(pause)

TM: All right, sir, I'm gonna have to disconnect the call. Okay?

Me: Well, we'd like to talk about the... thing.

(pause)

TM: Anyway, sir...

Me: What about...?

TM: ...thank you for speaking, please don't text and drive.

Me: ...what about grilling, does it..?

TELEMARKETER:

HELLO, SCAMMER

CAR WARRANTY CALLS

MODEL T

TeleMarketer:
Hi! Good morning! My name is Sara from the warranty division. Can you please verify the year, make and model of your vehicle so I can pull up your file?

Me: Hi, Sara! Yeah, it's a '17 Ford.

LISTEN
CD 2, TRACK 16

TM: Okay, so 2017 Ford. And what is the model, sir, of your Ford?

Me: Model-T.

TM: I'm sorry, it's a Ford Model-T?

Me: It's a Model-T.

TM: (confused pause)

Okay, sir. So outside from your Ford Model-T do you have any other vehicle?

Me: I drive the Model-T. The crankshaft is really reliable, the crank start.

TM: (confused pause)

Okay, so that's the only vehicle you have, sir?

Me: Yeah, can you help me with a warranty on a Model-T, 1917?

TM: I'm sorry sir but, Model-T sir is not qualified for our extended warranty. Outside from that, sir, do you have any other vehicles?

HELLO, SCAMMER

CAR WARRANTY CALLS

Me: Yeah, let's see... I've got a Studebaker.

TM: Okay.

Me: Uh-huh.

TM: So that's the only vehicle you have, sir?

Me: That's not a vehicle you do what?

TM: Okay, so right away sir, it looks like your vehicle is not qualified. I think we'll all set now. Thank you so much, sir, for taking this call...

Me: I'd like to talk about my vehicles! Please.

TM: Thank you so much. Byeeee!

Me: I'd like—can we talk about vehic...?

TELEMARKETER:

HELLO, SCAMMER

CAR WARRANTY CALLS

CHILI CHEESE DOGS (WITH FRITOS)

LISTEN
CD 2, TRACK 17

Automated bot voice:

    Press 1 to speak with a warranty specialist!

Me: (Press 1)

TELEMARKETER:

    Hi, this is Mike from the warranty division. Can you please verify the year, make and model of your vehicle so we can pull up your file?

Me: Hey Mike, how's it going?

TM: Doing great, sir. How are you?

Me: Uhhh, my stomach is a little on edge today. I had like, 2 chili cheese dogs with Fritos on top. And uh... man! But you know, I just can't turn down a 2-for-1 deal in the Walmart parking lot. You know what I'm saying?

TM: Yeah. That's really good, sir.

Me: Ya think that's why my stomach is all... MESSED UP?

TM: (pause) Yeah, let...   (cuts off)

Me: Hello?

TELEMARKETER:

HELLO, SCAMMER

"SEXY MAN" CALLS

VERY SEXY PHONE LINE

Sometimes a pair of telemarketers will tag team you. Do they really think ganging up increases their chances of success? Not when they're on the phone with **Sexy Man**...

(on hold music plays – Warm-up TeleMarketer comes on)

LISTEN
CD 2, TRACK 18

WARM-UPTELEMARKETER:
   Um hello, Dick! Thanks for patiently waiting. Can you hear me?

Me as Sexy Man:
   (In a deep, fake accent like Middle Eastern meets Ricky Ricardo): Yes, I can hear you verdy well!

WTM: Yeah, I have your licensed agent with me on the line and is going to help you complete your quote. Both of you please have a wonderful day!

MSM: You have a wonderful day, too!

(man with an aw-shucks, good ol' boy drawl gets on the phone)

TELEMARKETER:
   Hey, Dick! How ya doin', buddy?

MSM: I am verdy well. How are you?

TM: I am doing awesome! I got some really good news for you down there...

MSM: That's wonderful!

TM: ...on _____ Drive. I think we're gonna be able to get you a really nice quote going for the auto and home insurance. You're with Nationwide?

HELLO, SCAMMER

"SEXY MAN" CALLS

MSM: I cannot waaaait.

TM: Perfect, perfect! You're our kind of guy! Uh, if I was able to get you something better than Nationwide, would you be interested in switchin'?

MSM: Of course. But let me tell you something verrrdy important, though. You have a <u>wonderful</u> voice! Has anybody told you that before?

(pause)

TM: I have not been told that before. No, I haven't.

MSM: Yeeeessss.

TM: You're the first. I really appreciate that.

MSM: The best voice I've ever heard on the phone. Absolutely wonderful.

TM: Thank you!

MSM: Yeeessss.

TM: Thank you! I appreciate it! Maybe one day I'll go into recording the news or something.

MSM: Well, let me tell you somesing verdy important. You see, I run a phone line, and I think your voice be *perfect* for my phone line.

TM: Oh yeah?

MSM: Yeeessss. You see, it's a phone line where you **talk sexy to the ladies**. I think you be *perrrrfect* for it!

TM: Ooohhh.

MSM: Yeeeessss. Will you come work for me?

TM: (pause) Uuuuuaaaahhh. I dunno know about that, buddy...

MSM: I show you how! No, no, I <u>train</u> you! I get you... You make so much money you won't know what to dooooooo. Ladies, they go <u>cdrazy</u> for you!

(pause)

HELLO, SCAMMER

"SEXY MAN" CALLS

TM: Yeah, that sounds pretty nice, man. Ahhhhh, I got enough ladies on my hip right now, so… (lets out huge laugh)

MSM: No. You don't have to <u>take</u> the ladies, you just have to <u>talk</u> to them! They pay 100 dollars, 200 dollars a minute. All you do is just talk sexy to them!
I show you how.

(pause)

TM: (thinking) Hmm. Hmmm…

MSM: You come work for me.

(pause)

TM: All right, um…

MSM: Okay! You do this – you say this, Okay?...
"**I would like to see the caboose!**" Say that.

(shocked pause)

TM: (laughs hysterically) I can't say that!

MSM: Go! Try it! Oh, it is innocent! Go on…
"**I would like to see the caboose!**"

TM: I'll tell you this much. If you get a quote, then I will… I will… uh, look into it.

MSM: Oooh, but you won't need to work there anymore. Don't tell them, but you won't need to work there anymore ever again. Once you get this job you make so much money you won't know what to dooooo.

(pause)

TM: I appreciate the offer. I really do. Ummm, but you know, God's been so good to me. All I need is, you know, enough to get me by. So…

MSM: Oh, well donate the rest to charity then!

TM: (chuckles) Yeah.

HELLO, SCAMMER

"SEXY MAN" CALLS

MSM: Yeeesssss. Cuz if you do this for the ladies, the ladies they appreciate you so muuuuuch. You know they go CDRAZY for you!

TM: Already got enough ladies, man. Most women are a dime a dozen, man.

MSM: No, these are 100 dollars per minute! Ohh, you see this *different*!

TM: Yeah. What's the name of your business?

MSM: "Very Sexy Phone Line." It's a 900 line. The ladies call from all over the world. Yes. They go CDRAZY!

TM: It's called "Very Sexy Phone Line"?

MSM: Yeeeessss.

(pause)

TM: Hmmmm.

MSM: Try it! Try to say the line. I show you how to make your voice even sexier!

TM: Okay. Well, I...

MSM: "**Would you like to see the caboose?**"

TM: ...I appreciate it. I really do...

MSM: "**Caboooooose.**"

TM: ...but, I guess you're not into, uhh, the auto quote.

MSM: "**Caboooooose.**" Say, "**I would like to see the caboooooose.**"

(pause)

TM: I don't know that word means, so I can't say it on a... uhhm... (thinking) a on recorded line. So...

MSM: (innocently): Ooooh, it's just a word, it's on a part of the train! That's all. You see?

TM: (chuckles) Yeah, yeah. Yup. "**Cabooose...**" Yeah.

MSM: Yeah there! See, see? Yeah! Very good. Okay.

HELLO, SCAMMER

"SEXY MAN" CALLS

Now. Now you say it more like, "**Cabooooooooooooooose**."

TM: (laughs hysterically) No! It means the other thing! I know what it means in slang.

But all right, man. Well. (clears throat) I appreciate you. I really appreciate you. Ummmm... If you ever need a quote just let us know, Okay?

MSM: You have a wonderful voice.

TM: All right. Well thank you, man. I appreciate you and I hope you have a good rest of your day.

MSM: "I want to see the **caboooooooo**..."

TELEMARKETER:

HELLO, SCAMMER

"SEXY MAN" CALLS

LET ME HEAR YOUR SEXY VOICE

LISTEN
CD 2, TRACK 19

Sexy Man from the previous call makes a glorious return. And these property buyer scammers are not happy about it.

PROPERTY BUYER SCAMMER:
   I was wanting to speak to Patricia _____.

Me as Sexy Man:
   Yessssss.

PBS: All right. This is Adam. I was interested in your property on _____ Drive in _____ and I was wondering if you'd accept a cash offer on that.

MSM: Yes, I'd be very interested in that.

PBS: All righty. And what kind of condition is the property in?

Me: It is very good condition. You will very much like it!

PBS: (repeating back while typing this info in the background): Very good condition.
   Have you guys done any renovations in the past 5, 10 years on there?

MSM: Yes, it is in tip-top shape. We've done many upgrades.

PBS: (more typing)....
   What kind of renovations have you done on the place?

MSM: New kitchens, new bathrooms. But let me tell you something very important.

PBS: Okay.

MSM: To do business with someone I must trust them first. Do you understand?

HELLO, SCAMMER

"SEXY MAN" CALLS

PBS: Trust them?

MSM: Yes, and there is one way I know that I can trust somebody. And that is if I hear you say it in your **sexy voice**.

PBS: (pause)
(talking to someone off the phone – must have been a lackey in training): He told me to give him my **sexy voice**.

MSM: Yesss! Let me hear your **sexy voice**.

PBS: (chatters off phone with someone else)
(back on with me): Are you being serious, man?

MSM: Yessssss.

PBS: (mimicking me): Yessssss. Is that good for you ya? (laughs off phone)

MSM: Not bad. Now tell me your offer in your **sexy voice**.

PBS: (long pause, more chattering off phone with someone else): Maybe I could just tell him to go f___ himself, right?

MSM: (overhearing it):
That does not sound like your sexy voice!

PBS: (another pause, talking to someone off phone):
Does this seem like... fake?
(more talking off phone, and making unusual noises)

MSM: Why are you making fart sounds?

PBS: (pause, more talking with someone off phone)
(back on): Are you actually interested in selling your house, sir?

MSM: Yes, but that is not your **sexy voice**!

PBS: It's not my **sexy voice**?

MSM: No. I do not trust you!

PBS: (more talking with someone off phone): He... he's like Russian.
(more off-phone discussion, then back on):
Why are you so f__ing weird, man?

HELLO, SCAMMER

"SEXY MAN" CALLS

MSM: Who is the weird one? You called me!

PBS: You were asking to give you an offer in a **sexy voice**. I gave you your offer. I gave you 115.

MSM: It's not very **sexy**-sounding!

PBS: That's my **sexy voice**. I'm a dom.

MSM: I am not convinced, though. I must hear more.

PBS: (pausing again, typing sounds, talking with someone off phone)

MSM: My cat has a **sexier voice** than you!

PBS:

HELLO, SCAMMER

"SEXY MAN" CALLS

COMMUNICATION PROBLEM

AUDIO ONLY

You'll hear why this one is audio only...

LISTEN
CD 2, TRACK 20

TELEMARKETER:

HELLO, SCAMMER

Sometimes it's as simple as this to get rid of them...

TELEMARKETER:

Thank you for responding card services. How are you doing today?

Me: Hello, Scammer. How are you?

(pause)

TELEMARKETER:

LISTEN
CD 2, TRACK 21

THE EMAILS

THE EMAILS

I have a confession. When checking email I first exuberantly go to my spam/junk folder. Awaiting me are usually some juicy scam emails begging and pleading, "Would you mess with me? *Please*?" Munificent as I am, of course I oblige. Besides, is there anything more gratifying than razzing scammers until they realize *they* have been had? As they slink away seething mad, let us celebrate with a victorious toss around the horn.

That said, all email correspondence in this book is real. Nothing is scripted or involves setups, friends or cooperative parties. The scammers initiated all of these emails. Like the calls, the goal is to keep them corresponding as long as possible, wasting as much of their time and effort as can be liberated from them. And like the calls, it is **always** the scammers who end up terminating communication (sometimes in other languages). Scammers' emails here are reproduced as is – typos, punctuation and other errors left uncorrected. Mine, too – don't judge!

Now, let's mess...

HELLO, SCAMMER

Italian Heiress Maria

From: Khaireeman Shah Aman Shah
To: Me
Subject: Picked!
Sent: November 13, 3:09 PM
    @hotmail.com

You got picked to receive a Donation. Email: ASAP for more details

---

From: Me
To: Khaireeman Shah Aman Shah
Subject: Re: Picked!
Sent: November 13, 4:34 PM

Hey Kharieeman Shah Aman Shah! I love that you have two "Shah's" in your name. Can I just call you "'Man" for short?

What's my Donation? So exciting!!

From: Maria F. Fisolo
To: Me
Subject: Re: Picked!
Sent: November 14, 7:34 AM

Dear Friend,

I appreciate you for writing back as I have expected. I got your email from a web journal and felt strongly to write to you. I might not know your present condition and what you are going through in life, but I believe that this money will be of good help to you and your family. I am Maria Franca Fissolo, the wife of late Michele Ferrero. I am an Italian Citizen, 76 years of age, and worth US$26.2 billion Dollars you can also confirm from: https://en.wikipedia.org/wiki/Maria_Franca_Fissolo

The intention of this email is to be of immense blessing to people, at my age, I cannot continue to amass wealth without giving out. I might not have the liberty of time due to my ailment (Dementia in head injury and

HELLO, SCAMMER

Attention deficit hyperactivity disorder (ADHD)), therefore, I am doing this now. I have handed all my wealth to my only son and grand children, but there is part of it which nobody is aware of. I have been putting it away for this purpose since a long time now. I want to cede it out as a gift for you to help Orphanages homes in your country, and hoping it would be of help to you and others too, as this is my last wish to appreciate God for his grace upon my life. I would have done this myself but for my health reason and if I do it through my only son, Giovanni Ferrero, I am very certain he will not help anyone with it. Paola Rossi my son's wife succeeded in turning my son against me, my wish and dragging me to court the last time I gave out money out of generosity. I have made life worth living for myself and my family okay, it is my hope that you are able to receive this money, all I want from you is to be honest with me and help others from it too. It is my hope that you are able to receive this money, all I want from you is to be honest with me and help others from it too. One can never put a price tag on the feeling of doing genuine good deeds without any consideration of recompense.

As I wait for your response, I wish you a wonderful day.

Yours Faithfully,
Maria Franca Fissolo

From: Me
To: Maria F. Fisolo
Subject: **Re: Picked!**
Sent: November 14, 5:31 PM

Hey Maria! It's me, Alice. Alice Walton! That's sooo weird that you go by Kharieeman Shah Aman Shah sometimes. I'll call you that the next time I see you!

That is SO sweet that you want to donate some of your US$26.2 billion Dollars to me! As you know, I am an American Citizen, heiress to the fortune of Walmart, and worth US$40.8 billion Dollars you can also confirm from: https://en.wikipedia.org/wiki/Alice_Walton.
I still got you beat. Lol!!

HELLO, SCAMMER

So while your US$26.2 billion Dollars is kinda chump change to me, I can always use more chump change! Here's an idea -- I'll use your donation to "take care" of those problem children of yours, THEN open an orphanage named after their memory. It'll be called the "**Giovanni and Paola Memorial Orphanage**". That'll teach those brats. How's that sound!?
Write me back soon Maria... I mean Kharieeman. Giggidy.
(Don't worry, your name secret is safe with me!)
Let's get this Orphanage party started!

Yours Faithfully,
Alice

The scammer wrote back
Let's get it ON

From: Maria F. Fisolo
To: Me
Subject: **Re: Picked!**
Sent: November 15, 10:52 AM

Dear Alice,

Thanks for the message, I feel happy to know that I got in contact with a billionaire as I am sure the money will be put into good use.

I don't like the name you choose to name the orphanage you intend to setup. Well, that will be talked about in our subsequent mails.

I had Kharieeman Shah Aman Shah send those mails because I cannot send that amount of mails via my computer and he is also the one that searched randomly for emails on the internet. He is an old friend of my husband.

The amount of money I intend to donate is **$7,350,000 (Seven Million, Three Hundred and Fifty Thousand United State** [sic] **Dollars)**. I hope it does not seem as an insult to you being a billionaire.

HELLO, SCAMMER

I would also want you to send me the following details so that I can give the details both to the bank and also my lawyer.

Full Name:

Contact Address:

Country:

Age:

Sex:

Occupation:

Phone Number:

Then will I give you a letter to receive your portion of the money from the bank. This is my personal money and does not need many formal procedures, some beneficiaries have received theirs. My only term is that you be sincere to me and help the less privilege people that's all

As I wait for your response, I wish you a wonderful day.

Yours Faithfully,

Maria Franca Fissolo

From: Me
To: Maria F. Fisolo
Subject: Re: Picked!
Sent: November 15, 3:32 PM

Dear Maria,

I feel happy, too, that we billionaires got in touch with each other! It's like when you accidentally mix pulp-free and extra-pulp O.J. together. My taste buds are all giddy excited by the unexpected textures!

I'm sorry you don't like my orphanage name. It is admittedly kinda subtle. How about **"Giovanni and Paola 'Swimming With the Fish' Orphanage"**? ←Now that's a more Italian!

Thanks for clarifying about Kharieeman Shah Aman Shah. You know me and Kharieeeeeeeee! (that's what I call him) go back a long ways. Longggg. We dated. He's got dreamy eyes. And a ticklish ear lobe. Don't tell him I told you.

HELLO, SCAMMER

I floss with $7.3M every morning. Don't get me wrong, I like floss, but could we add a few zeros? We really need to bling out this orphanage.

Full Name: Alice. Alice Walton. THE Alice Walton.
Contact Address: Come on, you know where I live!
Country: Jeez, I already told you!
Age: NEVER ask a woman her age
Sex: Really?
Occupation: Full-time billionaire
Phone Number: Kharieeeeeeeee has it

I'm really looking forward to getting your letter so we can open the Fish Orphanage. It will provide aquatic hope for all sea creatures.

Yours Faithfully,
Alice

From: Maria F. Fisolo
To: Me
Subject: **Re: Picked!**
Sent: November 16, 1:10 AM

Hello,

i just spoke with Alice Walton (The Real Alice Walton). Guess being a billionaire has its own privileges and got to hear directly from her that she has not been the one sending and recieving emails from me.

I argued with her at first but i later realized that even the name on the mail is Music Maker, so i guess you might be just a commoner who tries to make a living with music (i hope you could atleast be a millionaire in a hundred or two from now, lol).

Well the reason for the mail is to tell you that you dont have to bother lying as you do not do a good job of it and out of my kind gesture, if you tell me who you are i might still go ahead with donating the money

HELLO, SCAMMER

to you. i know it will definitely go a long way to help your music life.

Maria.

———————⋐⋑———————

From: Me
To: Maria F. Fisolo
Subject: **Re: Picked!**
Sent: November 16, 7:10 PM

Maria, Maria, Maria. What shall I do with you, my dear, doubting it is I? First my lovely, you should know that the real Alice Walton doesn't call herself "The Real Alice Walton." No. That's way too overly earnest. The real one calls herself merely "THE Alice Walton". Note the impact of brevity. No need to ramble on with "Real" this and "Real" that. Obviously you spoke with the FAKE Alice Walton.

And what's this thinking a billionaire can't be a Music Maker? Have you never experienced the sonorous timbres of equity analysis, or the delicate counterpoint of bond underwriting, or the perfect cadence of a merger acquisition? It's music to my ears. And should be to yours too! Makes me wonder if you're the real Maria.

See, the Maria I know wouldn't dilly-dally releasing the orphanage money. No. She would make sure the suffering fish* are taken care of! (*fish includes crustaceans and invertebrates, except for box jellyfish – they're nasty!)

Plus, you don't write with an Italian accent. So Maria if it's really you I know you'll come through with the money, like now! Itty bitty not-jellyfish depend on it. Don't make them cry, Maria.

Don't make them cry.

(Crying) Alice

———————⋐⋑———————

HELLO, SCAMMER

From: Me
To: Maria F. Fisolo
Subject: **Re: Picked!**
Sent: November 19, 3:34 PM

Maria, why haven't I heard back from you?? I'm concerned. I hope you didn't over-order feather boas and smother yourself unboxing. Again?

Not again.

Alice

That's the last I ever heard from "Maria."
Or Kharieeeeeeeee!

HELLO, SCAMMER

3M

From: Olga V. Vishnyakova
To: Me
Sent: Nov. 30
Subject: Re: Happy Thanksgiving.

Your life might not be going as planned, But God has not forgotten about you. Myself and Family have agreed to give 3m to you, Please reply back to verify.

                      From: Me
                      To: Olga
                      Sent: Dec. 4
                      Subject: Re: Happy Thanksgiving.

Hi! That's sooo awesome! I always wanted to have a company, and 3M is a fine one. When do I get my new company???
You raaaawk.

From: Robert Baily [same email as Olga]
To: Me
Sent: Dec. 4
Subject: Re: Happy Thanksgiving.

Sorry for the delay,
    My wife has always wanted to visit Poland and i decided to surprise her. We are currently in Poland right now for a family vacation and also i have made sure you can receive my donation from here not delaying my donation to you till i return back home from my vacation. Please understand that we are not just donating to you because we have more than enough. We giving out to your family is to pass a message to the world that we need one another to make the world a better place.

    Please try as much as you can to utilize my donation funds to you in a Godly manner and let people see Christ in you and your family, Be a blessing to the needy at all time.

HELLO, SCAMMER

Please contact my bank with the details below and let them know you are my beneficiary and i am sending them an email with your Full Name and Email so they can be expecting you.

Bank Name: Bank Pocztowy and Below are the donation Committee

Monika Kruczek z d. Jaros

Director of Accounting Department And funds Transfer Manager.

Email: monikakruczek.zdjaros@

Kelvin Wright

funds Transfer Manager.

Email: kelvin_wright@

Hubert Chmielewski

Executive Manager.

Email: hubert.chmielewski@

Tell :+ 1 5
Tell +48

Please contact them immediately and setup an account with the bank that will enable them wire transfer my donation funds to your account as i was told that i can not send out such amount directly to you without a proper business relationship or having a bank meeting with you which is you must have to visit the bank premises. They further explained that due to the increase in Internet scams and Money laundering they do not send out funds in such manner even if it is charity/donation.

Please get in contact with the bank and secure an account with them first before they can wire my donation to an account you setup with Bank Pocztowy and you can now

HELLO, SCAMMER

wire the funds to your local bank account.
   CONGRATULATIONS.
   Regards

From: Me
To: Olga/Robert/whatever your name
Sent: Dec. 5
Subject: Re: Happy Thanksgiving.

Heyyyy Robert! That's sooo cooool that you're in Poland! Did you hear about the Polish kamikaze? He flew 59 unsuccessful missions. lolz!! What about the Polish firing squad? They stand in a circle. LOLOLOLZZ!!!!

Ok but for realz now... You said you have 3M for me. Weird! Robert, since when was 3M in Poland?? I thought they were in Minnesota!?! What's going on, Robert? I'm so confused! And while you're answering that.. Did you hear about the Polish guy that locked his keys in the car? It took an hour with the coat hanger to get his family out. LOLOLOLLLZZOLOLZZ!!!!

Seriously, Robert. Lemme know what's up with my 3M company. Can't wait to be company president!

p.s. If you behave really good, I'll give you a job cleaning our toilets.

HELLO, SCAMMER

Lerynne!!

From: Lerynne West!!
Date: July 12, 11:04 PM
To: Me
Subject: Re: Congratulations !!!!

Good day E-Mail <myemail@myemail>
I am Lerynne West, 51 years old. By Redfield Iowa, single mother of three and the latest
Winner of around $ 350 million in Powerball Lottery, your "E-Mail <myemail@myemail>" was randomly selected upon my request that you will receive a donation of 700,000 USD, due to the pandemic round the world i have to give back to the society
especially to individuals affected financially since the outbreak of covid,

Please send your full name, your age, your
Address (city, state, and country) and your mobile number .
After which My representatives will issue your payment for the 700,000 USD
Congratulations once again.

Kind regards,
Lerynne West

HELLO, SCAMMER

```
From: Me
Date: July 13, 1:16 AM
To: Lerynne West!!
Subject: Re:
Congratulations !!!!
```

Hello **Lerynne West!** I so happy to hear from 51 years old **Lerynne West!** You are my favorite Lerynne West of all Lerynne Wests.

I so happy to get Iowa money. Can you give me tips for lucky Powerball numbers? Do you play fractions like me? I play "7/16" all the time! Maybe that why I not win.
You probably not single anymore with $ 350 million! I hope you no need to sell your three children anymore?

My name is Kazungula Kalahari. I 51 just like you!! I live in Botswana. I the only Kazungula Kalahari in all Botswana. So you send money to "Kazungula Kalahari" in Botswana and it get to me. How you pay the 700,000 USD? In $1's or quarters?

Word has it that Kazungula has acquired a few quarters and feels assured Lerynne will deliver the remaining 2,799,997 any day now.

HELLO, SCAMMER

The Good Sport

```
From: Garrett, Thomas
Sent: April 5, 8:11 PM
To: me
Subject: I wanted to touch base with you
```

Good Afternoon
My name is Tom Garrett and I am here locally with [local cable company] Business. I wanted to touch base regarding Phone and Internet for your business needs. If you are needing to set up new services/add services or moving locations. I can help! I can provide a account review as well.

Let me know if you need help on…
…
*Upgrading to Fiber…

Most people like to work with someone local- So feel free to call , email or text. I am much easier to work with than the call center.

```
                              From: Me
                              Date: April 5, 10:58 PM
                              To: Garrett, Thomas
                              Subject: Re: I wanted to
                              touch base with you
```

Hello, Thomas. Great to hear from you! I was just thinking about upgrading my fiber. Can you help me with that?

```
From: Garrett, Thomas
Sent: April 6, 1:56 PM
To: me
Subject: Re: I wanted to touch base with you
```

Yes, what is the address you are looking at for fiber?

HELLO, SCAMMER

```
From: Me
Date: April 6, 2:24 PM
To:   Garrett, Thomas
Subject: Re: I wanted to
touch base with you
```

The address is **1 Colon Way**. I'd really like to upgrade my fiber here.

* * *

```
From: Me
Date: April 7, 10:06 PM
To:   Garrett, Thomas
Subject: Re: I wanted to
touch base with you
```

Thomas, haven't heard back. Can we talk about fiber?

```
From: Garrett, Thomas
Sent: April 7, 3:26 PM
To: me
Subject: Re: I wanted to touch base with you
```

Lol… it took me a min.. I actual searched for the address.. You got me lol
Have a great day.

HELLO, SCAMMER

A Special Note About

INTERNATIONAL DATING SCAMMERS

Most International Dating Scammer emails are accompanied by pics of young women purporting to be the scammer, but surely are not. I suspect most of these scammers are actually men working anonymously from internet cafes. These pics were likely stolen, so out of respect for these ladies I have replaced and reproduced those photos with models approximating the original shots and poses. So should you encounter any of the lovely ladies depicted in this book, please know they are <u>not</u> scammers but awesome people helping us make fun of them. Our kudos to them!

You will note that these dating scammers often ramble on and on and on. We have chosen to include the entirety of their verbose ramblings unedited so that you can read for yourself how they communicate. Feel free to scan quickly through or past them, though there are often gems a 'messer' can latch onto to mess with them.

Your typical dating scam generally follows a predictable pattern. An email shows up in your inbox purportedly from a young, beautiful foreign girl who wants to get to know you. If you respond, the scammer replies with tropes about how she wants to leave her country to come be with you, sometimes even announcing imminent, unilateral plans to make the move. Wow! So, so flattering. The emails become increasingly endearing, yet remain generic and often non-responsive to whatever you write... until the talk turns to money. Of course, now "she" needs money. Then it becomes <u>very</u> money specific.

Unfortunately for these scammers, they were dealing with me...

HELLO, SCAMMER

SWEETUMS

```
From:    Woman Sweetums
Sent:    March 15, 12:22 PM
To:      Me
Subject: enjoy your feelings
```

Howdy precious,

Thanks so much for your response. I was very surprised and pleased to hear back from u. Sorry for a long delay. I do not often make use of this email address. I by accident made the decision to take a look at my email box and was gladly surprised to find the message there. I use a different e mail and i just utilize it to speak to my friends. I am going to send a detailed message from this email so you'll recognize it. Well, i do wish that you will still pardon me for this and respond to me back in the near future. I would like to become familiar with you more. Therefore i'm sure that there is so much of interesting things we can easily find concerning one another. i did assured you to mail u my photo so i am enclosing it. Allow me to inform you a lot more about me in my future message and also i will send out it from my primary e-mail address, I will wait excitedly for your personal mail. Wish you wonderful day. Take good care.
ps If you did enjoyed my photo and you're stillinterested, please, respond soon.

HELLO, SCAMMER

```
From: Me
Sent:   March 19, 2:51 PM
To: Woman Sweetums
Subject: Re: enjoy your feelings
```

Woman Sweetums! Hi! I didn't know Sweetums was a woman.[1] That's crazy!! But to be honest, the idea of a hairy woman ogre is pretty HOT! You're right -- I AM enjoying these feelings! Can I call you my Bilious Babe?

So yeah, I'm stillinterested. Can't wait to hear back from my BB. Kisses.

* * *

```
From: Me
Sent:   March 21, 11:13 PM
To: Woman Sweetums
Subject: Re: enjoy your feelings
```

I still want to enjoy your feelings? How can I feel your feelings if you won't let me feel your hairy back?? Please respond!!

Nothing further from Sweetums.
Maybe she's still shaving.

---

1   Sweetums is a large, hairy ogre from The Muppet Show.

204

HELLO, SCAMMER

ANASTASIYA
THE RUSSIAN DATING SCAMMER

From: Anastasiya
Date: April 6, 3:23 AM
To: Me
Subject: Why you have not answered my question?

I still do not have any new letters from you.
So what does your silence mean?
Do you not wish to continue our communication?
Or do you not wish our meeting at all?
Or did you not got my last letter at all?
Please explain to me what happens...

Anastasiya.

P.S.
Why you have not answered my question? -
What is your real name?

HELLO, SCAMMER

```
From: Me
Date: April 6, 3:01 PM
To:   Anastasiya
Subject:  Re: Why you have not
answered my question?
```

Anastasiya ! Hey! Didn't you remember that you haven't heard anything from me because I've taken an oath of email silence? Dang. Now I'm gonna have to start all over again! Don't tell anyone, ok??

```
From: Anastasiya
Date: April 6, 3:05 PM
To:   Me
Subject: Why you have not answered my question?
```

In letter I asked for the answer to my question about your name. Why you have not answered? – What is your real name?

HELLO, SCAMMER

```
From: Me
Date: April 6, 6:52 PM
To:   Anastasiya
Subject: Re: Why you have not
answered my question?
```

My name is Mudd. What is your name, Anastasiya??

This scammer is obviously oblivious to the historic slang

"My name is Mudd."

```
From: Anastasiya
Date: April 7, 1:41 AM
To:   Me
Subject: Mudd, here my home address...
```

Mudd,

I know that many countries are quarantined.
But this doesn't stop me from applying for a visa.
I will get a visa and I can come as soon as all borders are open.
Why am I wasting time?
I don't think it will last long.
Maximum 1-2 weeks. During this time,
I will have time to draw up all the necessary documents.
Here is my home address,
-

HELLO, SCAMMER

to Anastasiya.
Number apartment: - 3,
Name street - Voennaya 9/1,
City - ,
Region (state) -
Zip code -
Country - Russia.

In case you decide to send me a card or a hand-written letter.
Unfortunately, I can't talk to you on-line, as I write letters to you from the internet cafe and the time is limited there. I wish I could chat with you but right now it is just impossible as I don't have a personal PC. But I shall continue to send you email letters and pics. As I already told you I rent my apartment and I don't have a phone there. Therefore I can not call to you. I have already given my phone number to you. I hope you get it. But my phone does not allow calls to other countries. For the reason of limits here in Russia.
Yes, I am going to come to your country. Somewhere in a month. I am going to enter the University or college. I am doing all the paperwork for this now. That's
why I asked you about the colleges or Universities close to your place. So I could study and meet with you there. I shall live in campus. Do you want it? You want that I lived near to you in your district?
Do not forget to send me your photos.

As soon as I finish this letter I will go and have a short walk. You know walking is one of the things I adore. It is so nice to have a long walk and then find some small cafe and get a cup of coffee there. I don't have a car and I don't really want to have it right now. And it is too expensive for me. I have no money to buy a car. I have never tried to drive a car and I have no license. Walking is much more pleasant. Unfortunately, most of the times I have to walk alone. All my friends are married

HELLO, SCAMMER

and they try to spend more time with their families. I also like to go to the movie a lot. But do it rather seldom. Usually I go there with my friends, but they don't do this often. They try to spend more time with their husbands and children. As I don't have children and a husband, I try not to bother them often. Sometimes I feel rather lonely but I try not to think of this often. Any way, my city is too beautiful not to walk. My city is very beautiful. There are so many places of culture there, lots of monuments. It is very green. It is especially beautiful in spring and in summer time when everything is awaken after the winter. There are also many parks and we have one boulevard with fountains. And it is gorgeous.

Also we have some really beautiful churches. I am Christian but I am not really religious. I have my own faith inside. And I go to the church but do it seldom. I am not fanatic about this.

I like nature very much and it is always a please to go somewhere to the country-side and to spend a day there. I like picnics, camping a lot. It is great to spend a day on the fresh air, especially when you are with friends or family. I try to enjoy it every time we do it but sometimes I feel very sad as I miss not having my second half near. Well, I am not going to be sad, as I am sure everything will be fine. Please, tell me about your city? What is it? What's interesting there?

Anastasiya.

HELLO, SCAMMER

From: Me
Date: April 7, 2:18 PM
To: Anastasiya
Subject: Re: Mudd, here my home address...

Hey, did you realize that if you dropped the "A" and "as" and "ya" from your name you'd be "Nasti"?? That'd be so awesome.

So check it out!

I'm just about to move to your town! I'll be living at Voennaya 9/1, apartment 2. That means we'll be neighbors! I can't wait to borrow eggs from you.

From: Anastasiya
Date: April 8, 12:02 AM
To: Me
Subject: Mudd, Do you like my pics?

Mudd,

I hope you got my last letter with my home address? Do you like my pics? I have friend Vika. She is close friend. She makes all my pics. She likes to photographe me. It's her hobby. I like to pose her.

I decided to come to the Internet cafe again to write you. I already spoke you - I shall arrive to you in a month.

210

HELLO, SCAMMER

I still choose college in which I shall go to study. I shall inform you the name when I shall know. I shall know all the information in a week.

I am going from the post office. I decided to send my parents a letter. As I already told you I am not really in good relations with them. But any way, they are my parents and I love them. I also have a brother and he is younger than me and they give him all the love they have. They always loved him more than me and didn't pay much attention to me. My mum wanted to have a son very much and she couldn't get pregnant for a long time and she was very happy when she got to know she was going to have a son. Of course, it hurts to know that they love him a lot and are not very interested in my life. But if they are happy, I am glad for them. My last relations were 2 years ago. Unfortunately, it didn't work out as he was too busy spending good time with his friends all the time and he almost paid no attention to me. I was just like a beautiful thing for him and nothing more. Since that time I had no relations with other men. You know that I write from the internet cafe. I have to go now. People are coming and coming to the internet cafe and you know my time is limited (15min). Internet cafe is a place where everyone can come and use a computer there. We have to pay for such a service. It is not a library where you can use computers free of charge. When I lived in Australia I often went to the library and could use computer there as long as I needed. But here the time is limited as there are too many people who need to use them. Please, tell me about your family. What relations do you have with them?
P.S. I asked you in my previous letter to send me your address.

I want to send you a card and my picture. Or perhaps, I will send you a hand written letter.

Anastasiya.

HELLO, SCAMMER

From: Me
Date: April 8, 2:31 AM
To: Anastasiya
Subject: Re: Mudd, Do you like my pics?

Thanks for the pics! I'm attaching of pic of the pie I had tonight after I took a few bites. I always forget to take the pic before eating. Lolololzzz!!!

Yes, I'd love more pics. For the address to send them, didn't you read? I'm moving in next door to you! So you can drop them off there, or mail them next door. (Maybe you're kinda crazy like me, mailing a letter next door! lololol!!) I'll pick them up when I get there.

Does Vika have a dog? Dogs scare me. I hope she doesn't have a Chihuahua. They poop!

HELLO, SCAMMER

```
From: Anastasiya
Date: April 9, 6:52 AM
To:   Me
Subject: Mudd, I have bad day.
```

Mudd, Sorry for not writing to you for a long time. Internet cafes were quarantined. Now quarantine is removed and I will write to you often.
I am not really in a good spirit today.

I had a very bad conflict at work. Some people here in Russia think that if they have lots of money they can do and say everything they want. I had a conflict with one very rich woman at work. She didn't like the quality of the clothes. And was so rude with me.
But I am just a shop-assistant. I am not the owner and I just sell things.
Sometimes I feel that I am very tired from my life in Russia.

I have nothing. I rent a very small apartment and can't afford anything better. I get a very small salary and prices increase here every year. But salaries are still the same. I was shocked when I get to the store to buy some food yesterday.
They increased prices again for milk products. Milk costs about one Euro which is too much. For-example, my salary is 10,000 Russian rubles a month. That's about 120 EURO, so you understand how small it is. And a half of it I pay for the apartment. And what is left I spend for food.
Therefore I wish to leave to live in other country.

HELLO, SCAMMER

Therefore I save money for a trip.
I am just tired from a hard life here. And I want to move to a foreign country. I want to get another education, to find a good job there. That is why I am trying to get a student visa. I shall study and work. I shall work to pay training and my life there.
I haven't decided yet what University I am going to come to.
I am still searching information. I would like it to be close to you.
I am doing the paperwork now. And as they told me my visa would be ready in a month. But I don't knowthe exact dates. It is just the way things are done here. As soon as I know everything, I will let you know.
I want to have a more stable life for me and my future family.

And what is more important I want have a strong man near me and to have a comfortable life for us.
So I am trying to save money any way I can for my trip and studies.
Please, forgive me for writing this to you. But I need to talk to you. It is sometimes so hard to be just by myself. And sometimes I need a strong shoulder and a friend to cry and to get an advice.
I know that you are a very understanding person. So, please, try to understand me. You are my friend and I trust you.
Now I shall go to a bathroom. I like to lay in bathing with foam. It would be great to take a bath together. It is very relaxing. And I think it is rather romantic.
You want it with me?
PLease,let me know what you think of this.
Write me your thoughts and your dreams.
Write a replay to me. Your letter will make me glad.
I will wait with hope.
Anastasiya.

HELLO, SCAMMER

```
From: Me
Date: April 9, 1:56 PM
To:   Anastasiya
Subject: Re: Mudd, I have bad
day.
```

I'm sorry you're in a not really good spirit today. Have you tried gnawing on sticks? That really picks me up!! Throw in some coca leaves for a serious buzzzzzz! lolol!!

Let me know how you feel after a good chew.

```
From: Anastasiya
Date: April 10, 2:04 AM
To:   Me
Subject: Mudd, Do you like my joke foto?
```

Mudd, Do you like my joke foto?

In the first lines of this message I want to apologise for complaining in my previous letter. I don't really want to complain and I don't want to talk about it. This was the first and the last time I did it. I was just in a very bad spiring while writing my last letter to you.

Sometimes we have bad periods in life and we need a strong shoulder of a friend. I hope that you let me think you are my friend. And I trust you that is why I decided to share my thoughts with

215

HELLO, SCAMMER

you. If you ever need to talk and if you ever need a friend, you can always talk to me...

I have been thinking a lot about our meeting and I want to meet with you a lot. I am doing all the paperwork now to get a student visa. And I do hope to get it. So if I get it I will be in your country. and I think it is really a very good opportunity for us to meet.

Please, tell me do you really want to see me? Do you want me to visit you? Do you think that we could like each other and be together in the future? Please, be honest with me and tell me the truth. I know that you are being tired with this question. But you should understand my concerns. This is a very major decision to move to the other country.

Perhaps, you wonder why I have such a big desire to move from here. The reason is very simple. I have nobody and nothing to stay here. I will miss my friends, but they already have their families and they live with their own lives. I have parents but you know we are not in good relations with them. And I think they will not miss me. I have no good job, have no stability. I have no family.

It is very hard to live in Russia and I don't think it will ever be better. And I am really tired from this life. That's why I have such a strong desire to get a student visa, to come there, to get a new education, to settle down and already to have a family. I hope that you understand me and that you support me in my decision.

Please, don't be offended if I don't always answer your questions.

HELLO, SCAMMER

I do it because my time in the internet cafe is limited. I don't always answer your questions because I am in a rush when I answer your letters. I come here 3 times a week and have only 15 minutes to write to you.

I wait your answer on my questions... Anastasiya.

```
From: Me
Date: April 10, 4:40 PM
To:   Anastasiya
Subject: Re: Mudd, Do you like my
joko foto?
```

Yes, that's a great joke foto! Do you like my joke foto?

```
From: Anastasiya
Date: April 11, 3:14 AM
To:   Me
Subject: Mudd, like you!
```
Mudd,

Today I am writting to you why I am alone. I am so tired that males sees on me as on beautiful pic only but not on woman. I think that we have much in common and may be if meet we will understand that we are a good match.

I am trying to get more information about the student visa and I

HELLO, SCAMMER

am doing a paperwork that is neccesary for it. There are so many things that I should do for this but I think it is worth it. I am going to come to your country. I am sure I will get my visa. And I want to know will you meet me there? You are my friend and you are a very close person to me already. And I like you very much. I feel that there is something between us. I hope you too have the same feelings. Of course, I can't say that I know you very well. But I feel that you are close to me. I wish to know you better. I wonder how it can be to spend time with you, to be with you, to cook together, to have dinner together, to watch movies, to walk holding hands. Letters are good, they help to understand people better. But only meeting can show the real feelings. When you can touch, look into each other's eyes, it says a lot. Please, tell me what you think of this. Would you like to meet me?

Any way you can be my friend. I will be in a foreign country and I will need a person I can trust. And I trust you already and I hope you do the same. Please, think on this and let me know if you too want to meet with me. I want it very much. I want to see you in real life, to talk to you, to know you real but not only through the letters. I think, I can trust you?

I already wrote to you, that all my pics is done by my friend Vika. She says I have a beautiful body. She is a very talanted photographer and I like to be her model. She is my friend and is a very good girl. She usually takes pics of me. We went to work together. She works close to my place. She is a shop-assistant too. Also today she has made 2 pics me and my passport.

I shall attach to you it in the following letter. I will go now to get more information about visa. I am going to get very important information. I hope to hear good news. I shall have information

HELLO, SCAMMER

approximately in half an hour.

Anastasiya

From: Me
Date: April 11, 2:31 PM
To: Anastasiya
Subject: Re: Mudd, like you!

I'm so sad to hear you feel alone. When I feel alone I make a family of mud figurines and play Pachisi with them. Have you tried that?

HELLO, SCAMMER

Here comes the dig for money...

From: Anastasiya
Date: April 12, 6:49 AM
To: Me
Subject: Mudd, information about visa...

Mudd,
I have all the information about my visa now. And I will get it without any problems. It will be so great to come to your country at last and to see you. I even can't believe this could happen some day! Yes, perhaps, I act like a silly girl. But I already dream of our meeting. I try to imagine how this could be. How I will touch your hand, look into your eyes.
So now I have to do is to show them all the papers and to pay for it.
But here I have one problem. I tried to save money. But I didn't expect I would have to pay for visa so soon. I thought it would be later. So I don't have enough money right now. And I need your help in this if you really want to meet me.
I need 20000 Russian rubles. This is 300 usa dollars, so you better understand how much it is in currency. It will include medical insurance and everything that should be there. Perhaps, you think why it is so expensive. Well, sum of money includes visa, insurance, medical certificate and many other papers.
I already have got my passport for going abroad. I have already made it and have paid for it. But I didn't think that they would give visa so soon. And if I don't pay for it now, I could have problems in the future with getting visa. And I don't want to miss this chance. To prove you that I am real and I don't lie to you, I am going to attach you a copy of my passport. So all I need to do now is to pay for visa. And then everything will be done and all we have to do is wait for the time it is issued. I have only 7-10 to pay for it and I will get it without any problems. This visa allows me to stay in your country.

HELLO, SCAMMER

I also plan to work there while I study. I don't want to depend on any one. I will return back your 300$. I am asking it to borrow. I will work and return back it.
I promise!!!
I've got to know that the best way for you to send money through Western Union, MoneyGram, RIA or Worldremit. Please, don't send me money by regular mail. First, for sure I will not get it as they steal money and things here. And also it will take long time for the mail to come. And then I will miss my chance with visa already. So, please, use Western Union, RIA, MoneyGram or Worldremit for sending money. It is an easy and quick way to get it.
You already know my address, I've sent it to you already:

apt - 3, Voennaya street 9/1, ▓▓▓▓▓▓ ▓▓▓▓▓▓, Russia.
And my full name is - ANASTASIYA ▓▓▓▓▓▓

You better check WesternUnion.com or Riamoneytransfer.com paysend.com to get more information and also offices that are close to you.
Also there is an opportunity to send money from the credit card. You just need to visit any office of WU or RIA or MG or WorldRemit.
Or through the site westernunion.com or riamoneytransfer.com, or contact-sys.com, moneygram.com.
You even don't need to leave your place to do it.
You can send money to any WU or RIA or MG or WR of Novosibirsk.
Please, understand my problem and send me 300 dollars.
So, please, let me know if you can help me in this.
Anastasiya.

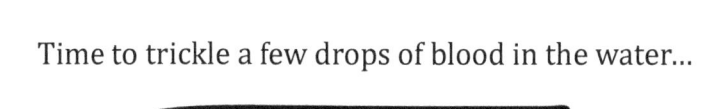

Time to trickle a few drops of blood in the water...

HELLO, SCAMMER

From: Me
Date: April 12, 3:33 PM
To: Anastasiya
Subject: Re: Mudd, information about visa…

I totally believe you'll repay it back!
So I just sent you 300 dollars[2]. Go check Western Union.

It worked. The scammer's tone changes.
Now it's all desperately about the money.

From: Anastasiya
Date: April 13, 12:13 AM
To: Me
Subject: I do not understand you a little???

I do not understand you a little??? Have you sent money??? If yes than I cannot receive it without your exact name and last name (sender).

---

2   I did not actually send the scammer any money.

HELLO, SCAMMER

And also without MTCN (Transfer Control Number). These are 10 estimated figures. Please, send me this iformation!!!

* * *

From: Anastasiya
Date: April 13, 12:14 AM
To: Me
Subject: **I need MTCN (Transfer Control Number)**

If you do send money, you would know that Western Union offers money without MTCN (Transfer Control Number). Why have you deceived that the money sent? you can send me a copy of the documents from Western Union?

From: Me
Date: April 13, 1:19 AM
To: Anastasiya
Subject: Re: I do not understand you a little???

I'm sorry, I sent it through Riamoneytransfer. My mistake. I threw in an extra 100 for the trouble.

> Of course, I didn't send "her" anything.
> The scammer fires off another series of pat responses...

From: Anastasiya
Date: April 13, 1:23 AM
To: Me
Subject: Mudd, sorry, I feel shame...

Mudd.
I do not know what to start my letter...
I feel shame and offended. I just want to tell you that I am completely serious. I have serious intentions to come and I am not going to lie to you. I am not a silly little girl that plays games to get money. Can't you see it from my letters? I asked you to send me 300. And I feel shame for this. But I had no other choice then

to ask you. The problem is that I have only 7-10 days to pay for my visa. I didn't realize I would Need the money so urgently. They took my papers and told me that I wouldn't pay in 7-10 days, they would just refuse me. And then I will not have another chance to get visa. It was a shock for me. I thought that I could just leave the papers and then pay for it before the trip. I think I would be able to find the money by that time. But it was beyond my forces.
I was shocked.
-
I went to all my friends and acquaintances. But all refused to me. They don't give such a big sum of money.
-
I don't ask my parents as they just don't give me money. When the last time I asked them to help me, they refused me. They told me they had to support my brother and themselves. It hurt me. That is why I do not ask them about anything any more and I almost don't talk to them.
-
I asked my friend Vika to help me, but she had not such money. She is married and has a child. And recently they have bought an apartment and took it in credit.
-
I also went to the bank to check there. But they even didn't listen to me. My salary is only 120 Euro. And they just can't give me 300.
I had tears. That is why I decided to ask you. And I feel shame for this. I understand that it is very difficult for you to trust the girl you have never seen before. Lots of Russian women lied to foreigners. But I am not the same. I am real. And I am not going to lie to you! I promise! I ask you this money not as A present to me, I am going to give them back to you. As soon as I come there and start working I will give you money back. I told you I was going to study and to work. I will be able to pay for my studies and for my accommodation. I already told you I was going to get a student visa. I will be able to come to your country and to choose any university or college. I can stay there as soon as I finish it. I am going to choose the one that is close to you to be able to see you often. I ask you one more time, please, understand me and send me 300.   Anastasiya.

HELLO, SCAMMER

* * *

From: Anastasiya
Date: April 13, 2:42 AM
To: Me
Subject: Mudd, another letter for you.

Mudd. this is another letter today for you. I wish to tell, that you did not worry for tickets. I need about 600 USD to buy tickets. But I don't need it now. I will need to buy the ticket when I shall receive the visa. I will try to find money by this time. I understand what you think now. If I can't find 300 USD then how could I find 600 USD. It is easy. I am going to sell my fur coat. It is a very expensive fur and I can sell it for 600-800 USD. I have already made an advertisement of sale. But I may not be able to sell it for some days. If I do not do it now, then they could just refuse me in it. Don't worry! I will have money for the ticket. I promise you! I already told you that you have to send me money to my city. You should use Western Union or RIA or WordRemit or MoneyGram for this.

And use my address that I have sent to you. You should send money to Novosibirsk for my name.

HELLO, SCAMMER

My full name - ANASTASIYA ▓▓▓▓.
ANASTASIYA - this is my name.
▓▓▓▓ - is my last name.
I already wrote to you, my address-
Number apartment: - 3,
Name street - Voennaya 9/1,
City - ▓▓▓▓,
Region (state) - ▓▓▓▓,
Zip code - ▓▓▓▓,
Country - Russia.

You don't need anything else to send the money. I don't know what else to say for you to send me money as soon as possible as my time is limited. Next time they will just refuse me in visa. I wrote you all the truth in this letter. I am sincere and open with you. I hope that you will understand me and decide to meet with me. Please, believe me and send me only 300 USD. And please, remember that I have only 7-10 days to pay for it. Anastasiya.

* * *

From: Anastasiya
Date: April 13, 9:55 AM
To: Me
Subject: send a copy

Ok if you have really sent money then send me a copy of documents from that as you have sent money. Then I shall believe to you. If you will not send a copy then you only play with me. I wait a copy of documents.

From: Me
Date: April 13, 4:11 PM
To: Anastasiya
Subject: Re: Mudd, another letter for you.

I sent you the money via MoneyGram*. Didn't you get it?

HELLO, SCAMMER

> *I did not send the scammer any money.
> "She" gets quite perturbed about it.

```
From: Anastasiya
Date: April 13, 7:23 PM
To:   Me
Subject: I already wrote to you!
```

I already wrote to you-

Ok if you have really sent money then send me a copy of documents from that as you have sent money. Then I shall believe to you. If you will not send a copy then you only play with me. I wait a copy of documents.

* * *

```
From: Anastasiya
Date: April 13, 7:24 PM
To:   Me
Subject: Why have you not answered?
```

Why you have not answered?
Please, tell me exactly if you have sent me money or not.
I have not understood you. I need to know the number (Reference Number) and also your full name if you have sent it. You have not sent me it.
So, please, let me know if you did it.

* * *

```
From: Anastasiya
Date: April 13, 7:25 PM
To:   Me
Subject: I need Reference Number
```
I need Reference Number

HELLO, SCAMMER

From: Me
Date: April 13, 8:24 PM
To: Anastasiya
Subject: Re: Why have you not answered?

Yes, I really sent it. I have made arrangements for you to pick it up. To get the money, follow these directions:

First, get a **pizza hat** like this. Then put it on and wear it when you go to pick up the money. I have told them to look for the girl with the **pizza hat**. That's how they will know it's you. You will then get the money, no questions asked.

* * *

A few more drops of blood...

HELLO, SCAMMER

> **From:** Me
> **Date:** April 14, 1:41 PM
> **To:** Anastasiya
> **Subject:** Re: I already wrote to you!

Western Union says you haven't picked up the money yet. Do you not want the $$$??

From: Anastasiya
Date: April 14, 2:24 PM
To: Me
Subject: I need MTCN (Transfer Control Number)

I need MTCN (Transfer Control Number)

> **From:** Me
> **Date:** April 14, 3:03 PM
> **To:** Anastasiya
> **Subject:** Re: I need MTCN (Transfer Control Number)

No, no. You need the PIZZA HAT first. Did you get the <u>pizza hat</u>?

From: Anastasiya
Date: April 14, 3:30 PM
To: Me
Subject: не пишите мне больше!

не пишите мне больше!

> [Russian translation: **Do not email me anymore!**]

HELLO, SCAMMER

That's the last I ever heard from Anastasiya.
Bye!

HELLO, SCAMMER

NURA

From: Anny
Date: May 7 4:40 PM
To: Me
Subject: You will be with me next to me.

Knock-knock! How ur health? It's seems you don't remember me. We've already corresponded to each other on the fellow neighborhood website.
Will you meet me?
I'm flying alone, are you live alone?I hope that your profile is true, can you tell more about u.I will be happy to continue our close acquaintance. Here is my new photo for you, send me yours in your answer please..
Nura.
P.S. You said you were good at cooking, is that true?

From: Me
Date: May 7, 9:24 PM
To: Anny
Subject: Re: You will be with me next to me.

Nura!! I remember you! Yeah, you're the girl who loves knock-knock jokes! You're awesome!!!!! So...

Knock knock.

HELLO, SCAMMER

Who's there?
Europe.
Europe who?
I am not a POO!!!

Lolololzzzzlollolz!!!

Sorry, I said my Aunt Naydgee is the good cook. I SUCK at cooking! I will BURN your cold cereal. I will make your PB&J sandwich inside out. I can't tell the difference between chocolate mini-eggs and kitty litter "goodies." Wait, maybe I am poo after all!!

Lolololzzzzlollolz!!!

Are we still an item?

That's the last I ever heard from "Nura."

HELLO, SCAMMER

LINARA

From: Linara
Date: June 1, 1:46 PM
To: Me
Subject: Hello

hello, I'm Linara. I'm sorry, but I don't know your name. please write me your name in the next letter.
i'm sure right now you're thinking about who I am and what I need. To tell the truth, this is the first time for me when I write to a foreigner on the Internet and even feel a little confused about how to start communicating.
In life, I'm not a shy person, but online communication is completely new to me. I'm a simple Russian woman who wants a sincere friendship.
Want to know more about your country, people, culture, and sport!
<u>Please tell me what city you are from and how old are you? Can you reciprocate and send me your photos?</u>
I live in Russia. I'm from the city "MIASS" in the Chelyabinsk region! This is where the meteorite fell on 15 February, 2013! I was born on 20 July 1990!

It doesn't matter to me your height, weight or age! Most importantly, your heart, your attitude to woman!
Feel free to talk about yourself.
I won't be able to call you at this time and I don't have whatsapp so we can't chat and exchange short messages.
I can only write 2-3 letters a week, because I have a lot of work in the summer months.
Perhaps you will ask me where I found your e-mail? 1 week ago, I accidentally found your e-mail on one of the sites, but now I cannot remember the name of this site. I'm sorry. I wrote you a short letter and I'm glad you answered.

HELLO, SCAMMER

Please do not ask on which site I found your profile. I really do not remember this today.
It does not matter and I do not know anything about you. Please don't think that I am writing you to get some benefit. No. I just want to chat, share photos, and stories from life.
This morning I woke up with a desire to change something in my life. I think that getting to know each other can change a lot. I know that many girls from Russia have found love in the US or in Germany, or in another country. I want to change my life.
Recently, I have been very dissatisfied with Russia's policy, it is very aggressive, and I often think about leaving here. or 30 years, I could not find a beloved man in my country, and I don't want to search for love in my city or even country.
I think that all depends on the willingness of two people.
If there is a great interest, I do not mind to meet in the future, but for now I don't think about it!
I really want to make friends with someone who does not live in Russia!
There are many cases when people are friends at a distance. I hope that you answer me and tell me about yourself!
Do you like football? Did you come to the world Cup in Russia? That was awesome. It was a real celebration of football and friendship of peoples.
I was not at football, but I watched the matches of Russia on TV! I would like to learn more about your country, people, culture and sport!
Of course I was a bit confused and I do not even know what to write in the letter.

HELLO, SCAMMER

I wish to tell you right away that I'm looking for in a man. I look forward to your integrity and respect, because I'm looking for love and a sincere attitude.
It is important for me that the man should be kind, attentive and responsive.
I will tell you about myself, so we can get to know each other!
I live in Russia, and later I will tell you about my own city, which called "MIASS". I never been married and do not have kids! I hope you understand me well, and the fact that I'm writing!
I learn English from an early age! If you only speak on your own language, I will try to translate your letter and we can have a chat!
You can look at my photo to see my physique.
My height is 167 cm, weight 56 kg.
I have many interests. I love books and reading! I read a lot of books of the great classics of the world!
I also really like the works of poets of the twentieth century.
Also, I like to listen to music. Recently, I prefer classical music, I like music from the 80- 90s, for example, Queen, Pink Floyd, Beatles. But I also try to keep up with modern trends in art!
I have a good sense of humor. I think in the future you will be able to see this.
I was born on 20 July 1990! My zodiac sign - Cancer! Which zodiac sign you?
I'll be glad to answer any questions that you are interested in.

HELLO, SCAMMER

I am very interested to know more about you, about your life, and the interests of the country in which you live.
If you are interested in our acquaintance, I am waiting for your letters and photos :-)
Please don't write short letters. Tell me about yourself!
Best wishes,
Linara!

From: Me
Date: June 1, 4:52 PM
To: Linara
Subject: Re: hello

Linara! It's soooo good to hear from you!
My name is **Чуйка на мошенников**.
Tell me more about you.

* * *

* "Чуйка на мошенников" roughly translates to:

Sniffing out scammers

That dispensed with "Linara" in one email.

Bye, scammer!

HELLO, SCAMMER

ALESYA
THE AGGRESSIVE SCAMMER

This Russian scammer wasted no time getting down to business. "She" lead with nude pics, a nude video and a request for money all in her first two emails within a couple hours. Designates me as "Guy" with no pretense of feigning 'getting to know you.' Gotta hand it to this scammer for boldness. But her impatience for money is something to take advantage of...

```
From: Alesya
Date: June 9, 9:19 AM
To:   Me
Subject: Guy, our first meeting...
```

Guy,

I feel like a fool. I'm tired of sex games. I will no longer send videos or naked photos. I feel stupid. I think that you don't want to help me. Are you superman or are you only virtual player? I will be honest with you...I really hoped for you and your help. Not very nice when your hopes are not fulfilled...Believe me it is not very nice! I was too frank with you. Now I regret it. I think you didn't like it !!
Today I learned that I had to pay for my documents in the next 5-7 days. If i don't pay, all my documents will be returned to me and I will not be able to get a visa. Therefore, if you don't send me money, you will destroy all my dreams... Because I think that real man who wants to see me will do all for this. I did all for you! You have seen my naked photos and video! Which I did only for YOU! I see you don't appreciate it! It really humiliates me. Only one conclusion - you only play and

HELLO, SCAMMER

don't want to see me. This is very disappointing because I so much dreamed about us, about our first meeting! About our first sex!!! I imagined how we would be in my favorite pose (____).

I dreamed that with you I would try my first (____) sex. Because I never had it. I want that all in my life to come true! And didn't remain only my dream! Please, help me, if you want this too! Sometime I feel like whore, because I made a naked photo and video. But I will not do this anymore. I don't want humiliation. I made these photos first time! And I did it only for YOU!!! I hoped that you would help me come to you. I wanted to come so that all our sexual dreams would come true. But now I understand that all this is not real! No matter how many times I prove to you that i am serious, you are always unhappy.

Because you are just playing with me. Yes? Is it true??? I ask you for the last time - Can you help me?

You will send me money for documents. If, yes, after I will do for you what you ask. But until you send money, I will not to do anything. Send money and I believe in your sincerity! Because TRUE MAN will find a way to get money for his woman! If not, you don't consider me your woman.

I repeat that I have only 5-7 days to pay for my documents We have to pay for these days! Or I can never come to you !!! 320 euros or 360 dollars is not a large amount! Tell me truth, please. Do you feel sorry for money? Think, maybe I am much more expensive!!! Understand one of the most important thing I am ready to share with you all your difficulties. Not just sex. We will be together and I will help you. I promise that you will have a delicious food and your home will be clean! I will be for you the best woman in the world! And I don't care that we are from different countries or that our age is different. The main thing that we had a spiritual understanding. Now, your choice! - Help and send me money or finish our correspondence, if you really only play with me. Please don't mock me! Tomorrow I will know for sure... If you need me, you will go and send me money. If not, this is only game for you. I don't want to write anymore... I want to cry...

Alesya.

HELLO, SCAMMER

P.S.
remind you - My full name - ALESYA
My address: , Russia, Irkutsk Oblast, Vvedenschina,

My phone: +7(906
I asked for 26000 russian rubles!
26000 russian rubles - 360 usa dollars or 320 euros.

You can send money through any international system money transfer: Western Union, Moneygram, WorldRemit or RIA to my name in Russia.

* * *

```
From: Alesya
Date: June 9, 10:46 AM
To:   Me
Subject: Guy, video again...
```

I am attaching you a link to a video from my last letter.
https://cloud.mail.ru/public/

[nude video]

HELLO, SCAMMER

I want you to always be able to see me. this video shows that I am real!!! I am not deceiving you !!!
I really want to come to you. Please trust me. I really want to leave here. I need you and your help. Please don't leave me in difficult times.
I only have YOU!!! I don't need ANYONE ELSE!
I understand that it is very difficult to trust a woman you have not seen. yes, there is a lot of hype on the internet right now. But I'm not cheating. I am a real live girl. Who wants love! And who dreams of leaving here. Fate gave me a chance. I met you. It's a sign. I believe in signs. I would be happy to be with you. I will be your assistant, friend, lover. I am a very kind and gentle girl. I hate lies and betrayal. Therefore, I will never deceive you!!!!!
I don't know what else to write to you ...Please give me a chance, help me !!! I am looking forward to your reply...
Alesya.

```
From: Me
Date: June 9, 5:54 PM
To:   Alesya
Subject: Re: Guy, video again...
```

Alesya! Thank you for sending me your anatomy video! Glad to see you have all your parts intact!! Parts are good. When they're intact. Intact parts are good. When your parts are intact, that is good.

Does that make sense?

* * *

HELLO, SCAMMER

```
From: Me
Date: June 9, 6:01 PM
To:   Alesya
Subject: Re: Guy, our first
meeting...
```

Alesya! Hey!!! No need to feel stupid! If you had sent pics of mustard packets you got when you asked McD's for ketchup, that would be stupid! Lololzzz!!!!!

So I was just thinking... what should I do with these 26000 rubles I had sitting around. Then your email came!! So I need to send it to you!!! How do I send it to you?????

```
From: Alesya
Date: June 10, 4:38 AM
To:   Me
Subject: (no subject)
```

Thank you for agreeing to help and send me money.
I already wrote to you:
remind you - My full name - ALESYA ▓▓▓▓.
My address: ▓▓▓, Russia, Irkutsk Oblast, Vvedenschina, ▓▓▓▓▓
▓▓▓
My phone: +7(906)▓▓▓▓
I asked for 26000 russian rubles!
26000 russian rubles - 360 usa dollars or 320 euros.

You can send money through any international system money transfer:
Western Union, Moneygram or RIA to my name in Russia.

```
From: Me
Date: June 10, 11:34 AM
To:   Alesya
Subject: Re: (no subject)
```

HELLO, SCAMMER

Ok! I sent it to you*! Did you get it??

*I did not send the scammer money.

From: Alesya
Date: June 11, 3:23 AM
To: Me
Subject: Re: (no subject)

I didn't understand you. Did you send money? Or will you send me the money?
How did you send? Via MG or WU or RIA ???
If you really sent money, I must have a secret code to get it. You received this code when sending money. Send me this code.
Or send me copy of all documents you received when you sent me money.

From: Me
Date: June 11, 2:01 PM
To: Alesya
Subject: Re: (no subject)

Yes, I send you money! It at WU!! You must go in person to pick up it. Secret code is...
8008675309[1]

I told them, Look for most beautiful woman in orb! Then you give her the money.
You tell me when you get there, and I send you something extra, too! Go. You go NOW.

---

[1] 800 toll-free + 867-5309 (Tommy Tutone) = prank phony number. Scammer didn't catch it.

HELLO, SCAMMER

* * *

> From: Me
> Date: June 12, 1:51 PM
> To: Alesya
> Subject: Re: (no subject)

Hey! Did you get the money yet? I can't wait to meet you!!!

From: Alesya
Date: June 14, 5:17 AM
To: Me
Subject: Re: (no subject)

I have not received your money.
I was in WU and they told me that there was no money
MTCN - 8008675309. You lied to me?
They said that I can check all information about money on their site -
https://www.westernunion.com/global-service/track-transfer.
I checked. And there is no money.
Please send me a receipt.

> From: Me
> Date: June 14, 1:36 PM
> To: Alesya
> Subject: Re: (no subject)

There's <u>definitely</u> money there for you. And a little extra more than you asked.
I think you're at the wrong store. Send me a pic of the lobby where you went. I'll tell you if it's the right one.
Hurry. I want to see you soon!!

HELLO, SCAMMER

```
From:    Alesya
Date:    June 14, 2021 2:23 PM
To:      Me
Subject: Guy, information.
```

Guy, I remind you once again –

remind you - My full name - ALESYA ███████.
My address: ███████, Russia, Irkutsk Oblast, Vvedenschina, ███████
███
My phone: +7(906) ███████
I asked for 26000 russian rubles!
26000 russian rubles - 360 usa dollars or 320 euros.

You can send money through any international system money transfer: Western Union, WorldRemit, MoneyGram or RIA to my name in Russia.
There are 4 of the most popular money transfer systems in Russia.
- www.westernunion.com
- www.contact-sys.com
- www.riamoneytransfer.com
- www.moneygram.com

Here are addresses of branches in Irkutsk where I can get your money:
WESTERN UNION:
Bank Uralsib
664003, Russia, Irkutsk region, Irkutsk, Gorkogo street 42.
WORLDREMIT:
AVANGARD BANK
664003, Russia, Irkutsk region, Irkutsk, dzerzhinskogo street 20.
RIA:
AO KB Poidem (Zolotaya Korona), Irkutsk, Russia.
MONEYGRAM:
664050, Russia, Irkutsk region, Irkutsk, Baikalskaya street 292.
Alesya.

HELLO, SCAMMER

```
From: Me
Date: June 14, 7:24 PM
To:   Alesya
Subject: Re: Guy, information.
```

Thank you for the reminder, Alesya! You will have your money soon, if you don't have it already!!

Yeah, everyone calls me Guy for short, but my full name is **Guyana Coop Republic**. Can you call me by my full name? Me likely that a LOT!

Guyana Coop Republic

> No response from the scammer, so I baited "her" with an intentionally very blurred pic of a Western Union money transfer receipt.

---

* * *

```
From: Me
Date: June 15, 3:21 PM
To:   Alesya
Subject: Money receipt for you!
```

I made picture of the receipt for you, Alesya! See, I tell you the truth! There is money, just like I said.
Now, do you believe me??

HELLO, SCAMMER

p.s. I'm still in school for focusing. Hope you can make it out!

* * *

```
From: Me
Date: June 16, 3:20 PM
To: Alesya
Subject: Re: Hi Guy, Appreciate it
and help me!!!
```

My Alesya, I'm told you haven't picked up your money yet. Is this true? Do you not want the $$$??
I thought you wanted to come see me!? [sad emoji]

Never heard from Alesya again. Bye!

HELLO, SCAMMER

LYUDMYLKA

> One of the great messing joys is getting scammers to say ridiculous things. For this Russian dating scammer, I got "her" to keep changing the endearing name she called me, each one more absurd than the last...

```
From: Lyuda
Date: June 20, 10:22 AM
To:   Me
Subject: Hey there my great pen-friend,
```

Hi sweet person. Now it is a great day for starting romance this adorable summer time. I am a unmarried woman. I am in search for a serious relationships and I am dreaming you too.

If you are interested Please reply ONLY to my regular email:

liudmylaonlyone@

Kisses, your Lyudmylka

HELLO, SCAMMER

From: Me
Date: June 20, 1:41 PM
To: Lyuda
Subject: Re: Hey there my great pen-friend,

Helllllo!! You have indeed reached Sweet Person. That is my name! How did you know? I too search for a serious relationships.

Thank you for beautiful picture of you. But sorry to see of your posture problems. Do you need chiropractic help?

From: Lyuda
Date: June 22 10:16 AM
To: Me
Subject: Howdy!

Hello!

What is your name? I have problems with my old mailbox. When I send you a letter, I get an error. Therefore, I ask you to use this e-mail. I am very glad that you replied to my little mail. I am very pleased to write to you in this glorious Tuesday. As you may already know my name is Liudmyla. But my friends call me Lyuda. At this time I'm twenty six years, And I'm residing in Ukraine the city is called Ternopil.

I am a student also now and I'm studying at Ternopil National Medical University. But more about that in the future letter. I'm sorry if my English aren't that great. I can chat pretty good English verbally, however, I make

HELLO, SCAMMER

errors while writing. It is better for me to have a conversation in The English language, so please lets write in English. Inform me much more who you are, all about your location, place in which you attain? This can be interesting to me. Based on your answers, I will see if it makes sense to maintain our discussion further more. But please do not get worried, I am not upset or whatever. I adore having a great time, I like to laugh and I have got a happy individuality. You will not get bored with me. I appreciate and love people who are close to me. In fact, I'm pretty decent and affectionate. Now hard time, and this time is called the war of our generation, war against coronavirus. On the one hand, I was lucky, because 5 years ago I made the right choice and began to receive a doctor's profession. A feature in our profession is that training is 6 years, and during the first five years we study all medical sciences without distinction, and only last year there is a distinction for the profession. I get a profession of a doctor of infectious disease. I love to be useful and help people in this difficult time of my vocation!!

Coronavirus, will be defeated, people will cope with this disease! When everyone is sitting in their homes behind closed doors, you still need to remain people and continue to communicate. A person makes a person with the ability to solve even the most difficult problems.

Before the pandemic began, I worked in a nightclub. After that, I had to change the place of work. And I started working part-time in the children's dance studio. I am choreographer and teacher dance classes. The most important thing that I did not throw dancing, as I really like to do it. The truth is, we are the builders of fate themselves. Can you agree with me? I have to ask you to read my own mail carefully, it can be essential to understand your thoughts and opinions regarding the things I m

HELLO, SCAMMER

sharing. It is simply my life sometimes causes a person always be very careful and inappropriate since of a good number of situations of fraud and simply nasty things on the online world. Who knows where our conversation will lead, but I really hope me and you are going to be at minimum great buddies.

Now I'm expecting feeling proper protection from someone, although I only count on myself. And it educated me to express joy in every single instant of existence, do not ever lose heart and soul and to never make a complaint about destiny.

I prefer that you're a true person, I want to call you. I would like to hear your speech and ensure that you are a real person. Write your cell phone number so I can speak to you. I have to claim right away if perhaps you just need my sexual pictures, and if i didn't interest you like a character, then please do not bother to reply. Many have tried to cheat me into obtaining my personal photos. Somebody stated the fact that he really loves me, by sending numerous kind comments, guaranteeing a lot of money, however, if I don't like a person.

And so the instant guys realized the following, they quickly gone away. It absolutely was incredibly unpleasant and attacking for me personally.

I am really not against candid shots when I want to, them to you if you want.I anticipate to see your email as soon as possible. I definitely will be incredibly excited to learn even more who you are as a person! I have a big request for you, please answer all my questions and comment on everything that you just think relating to all things I composed. It truly is vitally important for me.

Please do not disregard me, respond as quick as possible.

Best wishes! Yours Lyuda.

Bye.

HELLO, SCAMMER

```
From:    Me
Date:    June 22 1:50 PM
To:      Lyuda
Subject: Re: Howdy!
```

Lyuda! My lovely!! I see you still have the same posture problems. Makes me feel sad. Have you tried cracking your back?

Like I said, my name is Sweet Person. My friends call me S.P. -- "**Espy**" get it?? lololol.

Yes, we are minimum buddies, on our way to medium buddies. If we're in between, does that make us "medimum" buddies?

> Now that the scammer is calling me "**Espy**," we know that "she" is actually reading my emails and following my instructions. Excellent. Let's see if we can get her to change endearing names again···

```
From:    Lyuda
Date:    June 23, 3:14 PM
To:      Me
Subject: Howdy my friend Espy!
```

Hi my friend **Espy**!

I'm glad to receive a letter from you, and I am grateful that you want to continue our communication. Before I start write to you my message, I want to ask you, please read this letter very carefully, this is a very important for me, I want to know your opinion about all my words. Please, don't afraid tell my what in your heart and opinion about us. I always try to appreciate honesty in relationship and always tell only in my heart. I hate liars and persons, who put some masks to face. I am a woman for one man and if, someone will love me, then for me there will be no one man else. I am pleased to write to you in this fine Wednesday. I want to see what you look like. Send me your photo, please?

I'm not afraid of my work, I'm not ashamed of it. I like to dance, and I like

HELLO, SCAMMER

good music. And I have a beautiful body. I do not have complexes, and I think it's good.

Complexes make life boring. Just do not think that I'm corrupt. I am very vulnerable, tender and very true.In my free time I like to run in the mornings, and in the winter I go to the stadium to skate. In the mornings I always do gymnastics. I try to visit the pool almost free times in week. I very like to swim. During swimming, all muscle groups work, and this is very useful for well-being. Do you like to swim? However, I do not like it when someone starts bubbling in the pool, making a jacuzzi from the pool I hope you understand what I'm talking about. It looks, of course, funny, only the smell is not very pleasant. I hope that you're not going to eat lunch. Sorry if I was spoil your appetite. I just want to tell you, I really love life, and I rejoice at every moments. But I try to live with dignity, that I should not be ashamed of my actions. In fact, God sees everything. So I believe that I'm not doing anything wrong in my work and life. As you can see, my photos are not too frank. But with each following letter my photos will be more and more frank. As I told you earlier, I want to build only a trusting relationship and don't want to hide something from you. You always can ask me everything what important for you. As for me, you are very pleasant to me, it's very nice and grateful for me to communicate with you. I think I was not mistaken in chose you and I really want to continue our correspondence. I want to tell you more about me. I am 26 years old. I am an orphan. I have no relatives. My height is 171 cm. I weigh 54 kg. I do not have children. But I love children and in the future I would like to have two children (a boy and a girl).

Written you about kids and remember my not easy childhood. I grew up in an orphanage (shelter for children who do not have parents). It was very difficult years, it was very difficult for me. I'm terribly recalling my life in a children's shelter. Poverty, hunger, constant insults and peer bullying. It hurts me to remember these years. And I do not want to talk about it right now. All this is very painful for me and please do not ask me about it, I promises, I will tell you about this part of my life later, when I will be ready for remember this such a painfully years. But what to do, it was part of my life. But there are also positive aspects, At the age of 18, when I reached adulthood, I left the orphanage and started an independent, adult life. After reaching the age of majority (18 years), the state gave me an apartment and now I live in Ukraine in the city of Ternopil.

In the orphanage I studied perfectly, this set me apart from the rest of the children, and it paid off and I was able to enter the for free. Now I am studying at the Department of Public health. Next year I have

HELLO, SCAMMER

to finish my studies at the National Medical University, and very soon I would be arriving at your country to practice (an internship in the specialty of a Infectious disease). Only because of a problem with the coronavirus can my internship be postponed. Any way, my birthday is July 7, 1994 (Crayfish) and I truly hope all be ready soon and we can celebrate this important day for me in capital of your country together. I got an opportunity to pass an internship in your country for excellent studies at the National Medical University. It is a government grant that helps develop the skills of young professionals, but right now I do not know exactly where I will be in your country despite the fact that all my documents are ready.

I know only one thing, first, within two weeks, I must to get practice and accreditation in the capital of your country. After two weeks of practice, I can go to another city. As I know I would choose this city by myself, or I can stay in the capital. For the duration of the practice I will be provided with accommodation in the hotel and meals, in addition I will receive a good salary.Of course I had a desire to find a friend in your country, and faith smiled at me - you appeared in my life. Any way I will tell you all details about my trip when I will know it. For now all my paperwork is ready, so I'll be in your country very soon. My internship will take 6 months, during this time I will be in your country. I think that's good idea, we can meet in reality and have some fun. I would like to know you in a more intimate atmosphere! We can talk for years, but never understand that this person is the ideal partner for you, until we try touch each other. I do not force you to do this, because in the course of communication this will happen by itself. But you must to know, after the end of the internship, I must go back to Ukraine, in order to finish my studies. After finish my studies I want to sell an apartment and leave the country. My apartment is very small, but, no matter what, it is in my personal possession, and I'm very happy about it. Repair in the apartment I did according to my taste and desire. I got a very comfortable apartment. At least, this is my desire to have money for start new life outside of Ukraine.

In order to study at the university, I needed an additional income, so I worked as a dancer in a nightclub. I want to immediately explain that I danced only in the club and no more! I have no sex for money. I also despise these girls. I never agree with sex for money. Now I also need to do in a dance studio, but I really like it and I get great pleasure when I am dance. Because of my classes and work, I have very little free time, I rarely go home.I think that this letter was too big, and you are tired of reading it. So I will finish my letter. If possible, I want to ask you, when sending photos, you reduce and trim them, because I have a very slow Internet speed, and unfortunately I can not upload large photos. I'm

HELLO, SCAMMER

using the Adsl Usb modem. This system does not work very well, and besides it is not cheap. I pay for the downloaded megabytes, and if you download a large number of megabytes, it will be expensive. So I ask, please, reduce the size of your photos.

As I already told you, my Internet speed is very low. Therefore, it is more convenient for me to write to you only e-mail. About such modern means of communication as Skype, facebook and various kinds of messengers so far I can only dream of. The usual e-mail for me is the most acceptable and convenient option.

Please write me what you think about all this, I really would like to know your opinion. I hope you did not fall asleep while reading my letter. I hope my letter has lifted up your mood.

I'm looking forward to your new letter to me. See ya later!
YOUR LYUDA!

P.S I send you new photos and I hope that you will like it. It is important for me to know what impression you make on my photos, and I also want to see more of your photos, and I hope that you will send new photos for me.

HELLO, SCAMMER

From: Me
Date: June 24, 6:34 AM
To: Lyuda
Subject: Re: Howdy my friend Espy!

Lyuda! I'm so glad you got your back straightened out!! Did you do it like me, with dwarves walking on it?

I should have told you -- my friends call me Espy, but my REALLY good friends call me "**Tutone**." Cuz I got your number! lolololz.

And since you asked, here's a pic of me. I'm not very good at focusing. Do you have any tips???

Me, Tutone

The scammer fell for it and now calls me **Tutone**[2] ...

---
2   Back to borrowing Tommy Tutone's name. Sorry, TT!

256

HELLO, SCAMMER

```
From: Lyuda
Date: June 24, 8:34 AM
To: Me
Subject: Hey my dear Tutone!
```

Howdy, my dear **Tutone**!
I'm very happy to write to you on this glorious Thursday. Thank you for your photo.

I am very happy that we are continuing our dialogue. The most important thing is that I am very easy and interesting to talk with you. think it's important criteria for true friendship and even more love.

In my last letter, you probably have not understood my words about the trip to your country. I will try to explain to you all the details about it today. Please read my letter very carefully. Perhaps because of the language barrier that separates us, do you then can not understand, but I very much hope that we will find a common language.

As you know, I'm a Infectious disease at the university of our city. I am one of the best students of our university. I am a very responsible attitude to wards my studies, so I have a great chance of getting a gold medal, after graduating from university.

Only once in 5 years, among all Ukrainian students played grants to the opportunity to travel abroad for an internship (training in the specialty). Luck smiled at me and I got the opportunity. My joy knew no bounds. Of course, we had to try, because I have to not only learn, but also to work. I promised myself that necessarily going to win this grant, and I reached my goal.

I got a tremendous opportunity - I received a grant for an internship in your country, your country is chosen for a reason. Public health in your country is one of the best and most highly paid professions in the world, compared with Ukraine.

HELLO, SCAMMER

You probably wonder why I chose the profession? The answer is simple - this is my childhood dream. You know that I am an orphan, and in the orphanage I lived for myself, my caregivers did not care, because besides me there were still many children from junior to older. I loved to play in silence and independently tried to find a secluded corner in which I could read a book or draw, but I was not alone, I had a girlfriend, we played together. My childhood friend had a heart disease, there are special surgeries that allow him to be cured. Then I often imagined myself a doctor, I tried to operate on her, she was my patient. But it was only in dreams, in reality, she stood in line for an operation, but the operation was not all. But then, once, a foreign, childless couple was taken to her family in order to help and adopt. This often happened, usually foreigners tried to take children with any diseases, because in our country they were doomed. Thus, I didn't have a girlfriend, but I had a dream to treat people.

Profession Infectious disease is very important, therefore, the minimum term of practical training is 6 months. During this time I can get a huge "store of knowledge", from experts from your country. The most interesting thing is that the contract internship, my salary will be 2350 euro per month. This is a significant sum for a Ukrainian Infectious disease. On such wages can only dream of in our country.

I still can not believe that very soon I will be abroad, I have never traveled outside of Ukraine.

Under the terms of probation, the state pays for my trip to your country and a complete package which includes accommodation, food and clothing (if necessary). I am in no way going to need. I will be working as an Infectious disease physician in your country, and receive not bad money, which I will miss out on free use.

The first 2 weeks of practice I should be in the capital of your country, which will start a course of lectures. Then, all students will be in all the cities in your country and I would be terribly pleased to get it in your city, my dear friend **Tutone**.

I think it would be very nice to meet in reality, it's not always given a great opportunity. What do you think about this, **Tutone**? Passionate and colorful tiger cat - I think one of us could get a lovely couple.

I would be very nice to hear your opinion on this matter. I hope that does not make you weary. I want to keep our communication and become closer to you. In this letter I attach for you my photos. Please tell me honestly, do you like my figure? It is very important to me. If you want, I can send you a more intimate picture of the future. As I told you earlier that I did not want to hide from each other. I want to build communication only at 100 trust and understanding. I am sure that we necessarily will succeed, and we will for each other more than just friends.

I look forward to your new email to me. Have a good one.
Your passionate cat, Lyuda!

From: Tutone
Date: June 24, 2:38 PM
To: Lyuda
Subject: Re: Hey my dear Tutone!

Lyuda, my dear! Thank you for the new pics!!
Beautiful. You're still standing upright! Back boo-boos begone!!
I love your name, Lyuda. But can I call you Lie for short? It'll be my passionate cat name just for you!!!!

HELLO, SCAMMER

I'm so happy to know you're coming to my capitol!! You're gonna love *Amundsen–Scott Station*[3]. Can you cook for us there?

From: Lyuda
Date: June 25, 8:46 AM
To: Tutone
Subject: Hey my dearest Tutone

Hi, my dear tiger **Tutone**.
I'm very happy to write to you on this glorious Friday. I love animals, they are not able to lie and are always sincere. I like horses, cats, parrots, but most of all I like dogs. I think that dog is the most faithful animal. Of course there are breeds of dogs which may be aggressive, but it all depends on education and training master. Personally, I like the Husky breed. They are very beautiful and harmless. believe that this should be an animal.

I miss your letters. When I don't see your new mail, I open old letters and reread again. I am very interested to learn you better. Please answer me immediately as soon as you have the opportunity. I'm sorry if I sometimes not answer your letter immediately. Now I have a stressful time. We have to learn and to work as well as engage in my journey to your country. It takes a long time, but no looking at it, I find the ability to read your letters and write to your answer. I hope that you will not be offended by me, my dear **Tutone**?

It would be nice to talk on the phone and hear your voice, but to my great regret, most recently, I lost my personal phone on the bus. Buying a new phone in our country is not cheap. I think I

---

3   Amundsen–Scott is a scientific research station located at the South Pole.

HELLO, SCAMMER

can buy a new phone, during the passage of my internship, because the price of phones in your country is significantly lower than in Ukraine. Unfortunately, I can not give you any phone number. Therefore, the easiest way for our communication is currently e-mail correspondence, and I hope for your understanding. As I told you earlier, I have many concerns with the upcoming trip and there's no time to engage in a telephone problem.

Now, I do not know the exact date of my departure for training, I still kept in uncertainty. But, as I promised the University Rector, the matter will be resolved in the near future. Once everything is known about my trip, I will immediately tell you the exact news.

The most important thing for me is that very soon we will be able to meet, and I'll explain to you all, looking at your beautiful eyes. I look forward to the day when I can see you in reality. Mmmmm, it would be so great! Do you want this **Tutone** too?

Unfortunately, probably need to finish my letter. I want to close my eyes and dream of you. I want to see you in my dreams and make all our cravings, which are now only in our thoughts.

By the way, tomorrow I'm going for birthday of my friend Oksana. To be honest, I do not really want to go there. I think I would be bored there, because you will not be with me. Many girls will be with men, some of them have already kids. I'm tired of being alone and I want to be withs a man who will love me. I am very happy that we meet each other and we can develop our relations. But, I could not refuse my friend, because she is very close to me. I need go to her birthday party. All pictures done exactly Oksana and I want to tell her enormous gratitude.

HELLO, SCAMMER

I want to tell you a some secret about our friendship. When we first started at university, I and Oksana were lovers. We were young, we wanted to caress and tenderness. But our relationship did not last long around for 1 month. We realized that we are not lesbians. We have concluded that no one of girls would not give so much affection and love, like a man. We Oksana remained good friends. Perhaps you want to see her photo? Unfortunately, at the request of Oksana, I can not send you her pictures. She wants to stay away from our relationship. But I can tell you that she is a beautiful girl and most importantly, that she is a real friend who supports me in any difficult situation.

Maybe I should not have to talk to you about this because my story might not like Oksana, but as I told you earlier, I want to be among us did not have any secrets. This story with Oksana, was our secret and let it remain so. If you will not be easy, I beg you not to tell anyone about it. Let this story will remain between us. Do you agree, my lord **Tutone**?

I open your heart and soul and I hope that you will answer me in return.

I look forward to your new email to me. I hope my letter will not show you sad or boring. If suddenly you become sad, I want to ask your pardon for sending you my pictures. You forgive me? Once you feel sad or lonely, look at my pictures and everything will change. I want to give you a smile.

Please do not forget about me.

Million kisses for you. With the best regards!
Your holy cat, Lyuda!

```
From:    Tutone
Date:    June 25, 2:00 PM
To:      Lyuda
Subject: Re: Hey my dear Tutone!
```

Lie, my dear. Me so happy to get your email on this acrid Friday! I'm so glad you like animals. Do you like monkfish? They're my fave!!!

HELLO, SCAMMER

Monkfish – isn't he adorable???

Can I tell you a secret? All my girlfriends call me **The Regurgitator**. Will you call me **Regurgitator**? That would mean everythings to me!

But remember, very big secret. Shhhh! Like Oksana, ok?

```
From: Lyuda
Date: June 26, 10:01 AM
To:   Tutone
Subject: Hello my dearest Tutone
```

Howdy, my dearest Tutone!
 I am very glad to write to you in this beautiful Saturday. My sexy friend, very nice to hear from you again.

How's life? I hope you are fine.
I have great news, all my travel documents are ready.

Tomorrow or the day after tomorrow I am going to Kiev for further stay in the place of my internship. Literally as soon as I heard the news and immediately wrote to you about it. When I sit at my computer, I was hoping to see

263

HELLO, SCAMMER

your letter, and now I'm very happy that you wrote to me. I feel that I miss you already. Simply put, when I read your letter, my heart begins to beat in rhythm and frequent me on this nice. I feel the warm emotions, and I am very pleased to continue to communicate with you. Because I feel that you are very good and kind person. I am very easy and pleasant to write for you!

Oksana's birthday went well, but I was really bored, I was very sorry that you were not with me. Now I have nobody. And it is very difficult. I'm young and I also have a very large sexual appetite. Therefore, we have to settle for toys, dildos, and masturbating. I'm a little embarrassed to write about this, but I hope that you are not scared of it. I do not think I'm doing something unnatural. I just really want sex, and I need it. I think it's natural, and need not hesitate to do so. That is natural, it is not ugly.

Please tell me you want to see my new photos? I see that our relations are developing very well, and we can learn about each other everything. During self-isolation, people are forbidden to contact the outside world, go to cafes, go to school, or party. But the interesting question is how do people build love? How to find a partner for sex, sex is a great immune stimulant. And having sex increases health and reduces the risk of colds. I, like any other normal woman, consider sex as an important element of life, and I am a passionate girl. Sometimes in my sexual dreams I dream that I come to work in a doctor's suit, but I forget to wear anything under my robe and notice it only when I return home in the evening. My main feature is that I am loyal to a man who loves men, but do not think that I am too Orthodox, but I do not have any restrictions and complexes. Are you Tutone a passionate man? How do you feel about sex? I have funny stories that happened to me and my friend, although they are not decent to tell to an educated public. But I don't have any secrets for you. While I'm writing you a letter my sexual fantasy is so played out at least open a page on Pornhub.. Oh, wait, what am I talking about?))) Tutone, Although

HELLO, SCAMMER

wait, which section of Pornhub do You prefer?

I really hope to see your new letter soon!
A large number of hot kisses and hugs! With best regards.
Your kitten Lyuda

```
From: Regurgitator
Date: June 26 2:30 PM
To:   Lyuda
Subject: Re: Hello my dearest
Tutone
```

Hello, my deerish Lie! That's sexier than sexy that you find me sexy! But you know what's sexiest? When you call me by my sexy name --
The Regurgitator.

Please call me **Regurgitator** from now on, my deer, ok?
That's sooo hawt.

Yours only,

The Regurgitator

```
From: Lyuda
Date: June 28, 7:29 AM
To:   Regurgitator
Subject: Howdy my dear tiger Regurgitator
```

Hi there my sexy **Regurgitator**!

I am very glad to write to you in this beautiful Monday. I am very happy to see your letter.

You are very hot and sexy man, it can be clearly seen from your letters.

Now I collect things for my trip. My train to Kiev departs in 4 hours, and I need to check whether I collected all the things that will be

HELLO, SCAMMER

needed during the trip.

In the end, I leave not for a few days, I am leaving as much as 6 months. Therefore, I must not forget anything. Because of this, so many thoughts in my head and emotions.

I am very glad that very soon we will be able to meet in real life.

I'll be in Kiev for a few days, I need to handle all formalities, and then I shall fly to your country. I'll get back to you from Kiev. I think I can write you from Internet cafe in Kiev. It is much cheaper than calling. I have now is not too good situation with cash, so I'll write you e-mail. I am very worried now, I've never been outside Ukraine, and I do not know how you have everything arranged. Your rules of conduct, traditions and customs are still very much a mystery to me. But I'm learning fast! With your help, I sure would succeed.

I just do not know the cost of living in your country. What do you think, will I be enough monthly salary an Infectious disease physician in the amount of 2350 euro? In Ukraine it is very big money, but I do not know the value of the money in your country.

I think that we can spend this money together, because the money I receive as my personal expenses.

All other expenses related to my accommodation and meals are funded through the government's internship program. Do you think it's good money **Regurgitator**?

But now a little early to think about it. The money I will have when I arrive in the Lie. I already told you that should be in Lie for 2 weeks. I got all instructions in the Ukrainian embassy and the government will give me my first paycheck for the next personal expenses for my arrival in your country. After two weeks spent in the Lie I'm heading into your city. So I want to know all the information in order to avoid any mistakes or problems.

Please write me, how exactly is called your city, and what the closest airport to you. I'll write down this information so that I have not forgotten. **Regurgitator** I do not know if you have the opportunity, but would very much wish we could meet at the airport as soon as I shall fly to the Lie.

I really want to meet you as soon as possible. I am very excited with my thoughts. It's still just a thought, but I very much hope that soon our dreams will come true. How do you imagine our meeting? I think we could have lunch somewhere, then walk a little and chat. And then, I would like to know you more closely! I hope you understand what I mean?

Get ready, I'm getting close, you'll get a hard hot, wild sex, a sex that you had never before this! And please do not masturbate until I came to, I want all your cum! And now came to me, my girlfriend and I should finish my letter, it will help me to collect things and take them to the station. I will contact you and give you all the information about my flight as soon as I arrive in Kiev. I finish my letter as soon as read it, please tell me! I wish you good luck!

Even if I do not see your letter from home, I can read it when arrive in Kiev, and it would be very nice. I really wanted to see the answers to my questions in your letter! I kiss your whole body! Have a good one.

Your princess, Lyuda!

HELLO, SCAMMER

```
From:    Regurgitator
Date:    June 28, 2:41 PM
To:      Lyuda
Subject: Re: Howdy my dear tiger
Regurgitator
```

Hello my purge princess! Me so glad you find The Regurgitator hot and sexy man!!

First thing to do when you arrive is you must meet my friend, Chuck...

Up-Chuck.

Can you say "Hello!!" to my friend, **Up-Chuck**, in that sexy, hurly way you do??

I can't wait to see you in Amundsen–Scott Station. Refrigeration costs are very low here. You'll have chills before you know it!!

```
From:    Lyuda
Date:    June 29, 7:53 AM
To:      Chuck
Subject: Hi, my Tiger Chuck
```

Hi, my favorite Tiger **Chuck**!

I am very glad to write to you in this Tuesday. I am very pleased to receive your new letter. Thank you for what you are close with me. You're important to me and at this stage of my life, I live only for you.

Sorry, but I think we should end our conversation. This is a very unpleasant and painful decision for me. I do not want you to suffer. You became for me a very expensive man, but I see no other solution.

Now I am in Kiev and I am writing from internet cafes. I got to Kiev good, but

HELLO, SCAMMER

have a problem without solving that, I can not come to you. Because, I haven't small sum of money. For me it's a shame, ask your financial aid, and I will not do that. So, I decided to end our correspondence, because I do not want you to think about me is wrong.

I tried to solve this problem myself, but I did not get. I think that you refuse to help me. As I told you earlier, for this reason that we should end our conversation. I think you're going to accuse me and your confidence in me fade away. I do not want to hear the screams and insults from the person to whom I have a warm, loving feelings. My heart will be broken.

I am in complete disarray, my angel **Chuck**, I'm really afraid of losing you. I feel so bad now, I shake hands, and quivering voice. On my eyes with tears. I do not know what I do, I think you're not going to help me and you will reject me. Please understand that I do not want to hear it in my address insults and accusations. Please do not tell me bad words.

I look forward to your letter with your thoughts on the matter. am very afraid of losing you and in your heart do not believe that you refuse to help me.

You're a wonderful person, we have built huge plans for our future. Is this all just collapses in a moment? I do not want and I will not believe it. You should always keep a positive hope. I'm sure between us all out.

Do you agree with me?

During our conversation I am very much accustomed to you, and

HELLO, SCAMMER

I want to be with you in real life. I want passionate, to some extent wild, and longer sex with you, my angel **Chuck**. I am burning with the thought that soon you come to me. Now everything is in jeopardy and I am very upset. Probably, I was so stupid, thinking that was the happiest woman in this vast world.
I look forward to your answer. Bye.
Your passionate kitten, Lyuda!

```
From:  Up-Chuck
Date:  June 29, 2:14 PM
To:    Lyuda
Subject: Re: Hi, my Tiger Chuck
```

Hey hey sweet baby doll, Lyuda. It's Regurgitator's best friend, **Up-Chuck**. Remember baby cakes, it's...

<u>Up</u> - <u>Chuck</u>

Daddy likes it when you call me that. Just hoppin on my bud Regurgitator's email account to say whassup girl? Dang u so beautiful I might change my name to Ralph.

Gimme some sugar baby! Some of dat disgorged dextrose – **Up-Chuck** style. Please?!

* * *

```
From:  Regurgitator
Date:  June 29, 2:43 PM
To:    Lyuda
Subject: Re: Hi, my Tiger Chuck
```

Hey Lyuda, it's your hot heaver, **Regurgitator**. So sorry that Up-Chuck got on my email to contact you. He's either smitten or he's gonna hurl. Don't know why he won't get his own email.

Anyways. I'm here for you, Lie. When I'm in disarray I reach for *Kaopectate*. Works great for a few minutes! Have you tried that?

HELLO, SCAMMER

That's the last I ever heard from "Lyuda".
Bye!

HELLO, SCAMMER

ELENA

```
From: Elena
Date: June 29, 5:32 AM
To:   Me
Subject: Hi My New Friend, it`s Elena. I hope you
are not angry with me?
```

Hello again, it's Elena, I hope you remember me. I wrote you the letter a few days ago, but have not received your answer.[4] Probably my letter has not reached you, therefore I again send this letter, I hope you receive it this time.

Hello dear stranger How are you? My parents gave me a name Elena, Me 34 years old.

First of all I want to explain where did I find your e-mail address. I went to agency of acquaintance and said that I want to find a serious man through the Internet. I want to destroy the loneliness and to find the good person who, as well as me will want to share all pleasure of life. In our country many lonely people use such services. So they gave me your e-mail address and said that you are also trying to find a good and serious partner in life. I hope they did not deceive me, since they received monetary compensation from me. If it so inform me and I will not disturb more you. I think you would like to know who I am? And I would like to tell you. I am from a country called Russia, in the southern part of this country. My house is located in Brutovo - small beatifull village. I am happy to live here, unfortunately there is a problem. Although my country big enough, but there are no decent men for serious-relationship. I am a single wonderful girl try to find pleasant man for real love and relationship, who can really love and appreciate

---

4   This scammer did not previously write me, unless as another scammer.

HELLO, SCAMMER

own woman. Before I start telling you my story let me inform you about a very important fact. I hope you're not disappointed that I don't live in your state (I think you've already guessed). I sincerely hope it doesn't frighten you. I'm the same as ladies living in different state. I'm just a human being with a heart and soul. I suppose my nationality and location don't disappoint you and you will answer my answer. I think the nationality and cultural difference are not the most important things in a ladies for you. By the way in the nearest future I'm going to travel. Maybe I visit your state and who knows we are possibly become friends or maybe even more… and if your interest isn't limited only by distance and boundaries I'll be really happy.

Now let me tell you a few words about myself. I live in Russia. The hamlet I live in is called "Brutovo". It's a small village where just 1300 people live. Maybe you'll try to find my place on the map. It's not far from Vladimir (a large city in the south-west of my country). In my childhood I dreamed of becoming an interpreter of the English language and I wanted to work with our President to know state and international secrets.(smile). But the fortune disposed in a different way. I started my education in a medical school. After finishing school I entered Medical University. Now I work at hospital. I'm a gynecologist.

New Friend I promised to send you my photo and now I keep my promise. I hope you like them. In addition I want to say that my hair is light though I change it sometimes. My height is 5 feet 6 inches. My weight is 125 pounds. As you know I'm 34 years old. I was born on May 15 in 1987. Of course tastes differ but maybe you'll like my pic and my appearance. In other case if you don't like my appearance please let me know, I won't disturb you any longer.

I should say I'm an optimist in the depth of my heart and it helps me in my life. I'm not a little girl and I see my life from a philosophical point of view. I can't make myself an absolutely happy woman. I've got a wonderful job and good house. But there are things that make people happy. They are not material things, they are more than that. I was the first who wrote that. It means I'm ready to share my thoughts with you. I'm very glad and grateful you've written me. In any case I hope you are interested in our dialog and I'll be looking forward to getting an email from you. At the

HELLO, SCAMMER

end of the letter I want to ask you simple questions. What is your profession? Do you like your job? Have you got an experience in communicating with people from other countries? Maybe you're more qualified in it than me. If you don't want to answer the questions please don't do it. It's just my woman's curiosity. I'll be extremely grateful if send me your photos. I'm sure to save them in my computer.
Best regards.
Elena.

P.S. Your answer went to my spam folder so I did not see it immediately. I was interested why. To me have recommended to place you in a "favorite list".
Maybe my email to you too get in spam? Place me in a "favorite list".

```
From: Me
Date: June 29, 9:22 AM
To:   Elena
Subject: Re: Hi My New Friend,
it`s Elena. I hope you are not
angry with me?
```

Elena! Hay. I like hay.

HELLO, SCAMMER

Thanks for the pictures. But I was hoping you'd be prettier. Can you get some plastic surgery or something and get back with me?

From: Elena
Date: June 30, 10:06 AM
To: Me
Subject: Hi my friend

Hi FRIEND!!! I do not understand why you have not written the name? It's a secret? Smile. Please write the next letter to his name. While I will name you - the FRIEND.

How are you doing? How did you spend your day? I hope you are glad to get my email? When I got yours I was in the seventh heaven, I was the happiest lady in the world!!!!!!!! Thanks a lot. Now I want to explain the fact about my opportunity to write you letters. I send my emails to you from my job because I haven't got a computer at home. The computer I use is in the Accountant Department. The lady who works with the computer lets me use it for my personal purposes sometimes. It depends not only from me and my desires, unfortunately.

I work from Monday till Friday. It's Russian standard. That's why I won't be able to send and get emails on Saturday and Sunday. But sometimes I have to work at weekends because any pain hasn't got a schedule. (smile) I suppose you remember I'm a gynecologist. That's why I will have an opportunity to write you on Saturday and Sunday.

Thanks for the answer. Before we begin our correspondence, I

HELLO, SCAMMER

would like to know your name. As for my work, I makes survey of the person, definition of symptoms of illness, installation of the exact diagnosis, assignment of analyses, the analysis of results of surveys and analyses, define course of treatment and makes a decision on surgical intervention. I don't do plastic surgery.I am a female gynecologist.

I wanted to ask you a question. In which city do you live? This is a big city or small?

What is the name of your city?

Now I'm going to tell you about my interests. My hobby let me say so is the English language. I have been interested in it for so long since my school years. The educational program in Russia includes learning foreign languages. As a rule they are English, German and French. I started learning English and now I'm extremely happy that I made the right choice. I absolutely love the English language. After finishing school I continued learning the language at the University. I had been learning English for 18 years. I want to know it perfectly. I speak English. Maybe you'll like my accent (Russian I mean) I have. It's possible there are some mistakes in the text but I'm sure you won't offend.

Another hobby I have is knitting. It's the deal of my life. My mum taught me how to knit in my childhood and now I knit clothes (sweaters, jackets and waistcoats) for my friends and myself. I adore knitting and I like wearing woolen clothes. Almost all warm clothes I have got I've knitted myself. I don't know if knitting is popular in your country as for Russia it's really fashionable and up to date. What else can I tell you about my life? I haven't got children, I've never been married. Of course I had relations with men I even thought that they were serious and would last long

HELLO, SCAMMER

and come to marriage but I was mistaken. Now I have got nothing but bad and painful memories.

FRIEND, how can you describe your character? As for me I've never tried to describe the traits of my character but nevertheless I'll try. I live with a smile on my face and a hope in my heart. I consider myself an optimist. And maybe it helped me be the first to write. I've seen and experienced a lot in my life. During 34 years I'd been overcome a lot of difficulties. You know I don't need much in my life to be happy. All I need is a real man who will be my friend, my love and support forever. And it happened so that now I'm looking for him in such a way. I don't think it's wrong. And what do you think of it? I live honestly and it brings me satisfaction and pleasure. I know happiness doesn't need a lot. Maybe the most essential thing I lack now is love. A human being can't be happy without love. I mean not only love between a man and woman but also love to the family. For instance, I haven't got a family and it really oppresses and depresses me.

FRIEND, do you often meet your relatives? I really miss the time when I had a lot of relatives. I want to return it. Are you looking for a soul mate or just a friend? What are you looking for in the soul mate, FRIEND, if it is so? I hope to hear from you very soon.

Best regards.
Elena.

HELLO, SCAMMER

From: Me
Date: June 30, 2:46 PM
To: Elena
Subject: Re: Hi my friend

Elena, thank you for the picture of yourself. Did you get the plastic surgery since your last email? You don't look any prettier than last time.

And thank you for the map of your location! Here's my location. It's very quiet here, but super nice having a planet all to yourself. I'd invite you to come live with me, but not until you get plastic surgery. When will you schedule it?

MY LOCATION:

---

5   In case you didn't know, this is Mars.

HELLO, SCAMMER

Then another "Elena" showed up in my inbox.
Let's pit Elenas against each other…

ELENA 2

From: Lenusha <heather@
Date: July 16, 12:59 PM
To: Me
Subject: Destiny guides me...

Toc-toc. What's happening?
Iam **Elena**. Name your? and I am 47 age.
I am live Russian Federation. Well, when are we going to meet her?:).
Very glad to know you. I will expect an answer within 48 hours).
Have a nice day!

From: Me/Elena
Date: July 17, 1:06 PM
To: Lenusha/Elena
Subject: Re: Destiny guides me…

Elena? My name is Elena, too! But I'm prettier than you -- see pic. Admit it, k? Then we can be friends.

HELLO, SCAMMER

So why did you write? Hope you're not trying to stir things up, cuz you be goin' DOWN biatch!!

Elena

* * *

```
From: Me/Elena
Date: July 17, 1:06 PM
To: Elena
Subject: Re: Destiny guides me...
```

Я единственная, кого называют «Елена» по электронной почте. Отступи от того, кем ты есть!!

* * *

*roughly translates to...

"I'm the only one who is called 'Elena' by email. Back off whoever you are!!"

That took care of both Elenas.

THE SNAIL MAILS

HELLO, SCAMMER

THE SNAIL MAILS

SONG SHARK MAIL SCAMS

Sharks lurk the oceans for fresh meat. "Song sharks" lurk the songwriting world for the same. These "sharks" exploit the dreams of aspiring musicians who yearn for their songs to become hits recorded by major artists (or dream of becoming major artists themselves). For most writers, songwriting is an emotional, personal experience, so their dreams of "making it" is ripe for exploitation. Eagerness for success and fame can become muddled with potentially bad business decisions and opportunistic song sharks are ready to pounce. They take advantage these dreams by making grandiose but nonspecific promises of stardom, but rarely to never making good on them, all while draining their bank accounts. Song sharks get away with it because they remain "technically" within the law and the contract signed by the bilked. A long trail of dashed dreams and thinner wallets lay in their wake. Lest you may feel sorry for these sharks, a cursory Internet search for "Hilltop Records" (which we will get into in this chapter) yields reports[1] from victims such as:

> **I need abswer** [sic] **from hill top records for my song REMEMBRANCE i wrote and paid my money in 2010 and haven't heard nothing from HILL TOP records i need aswers** [sic]
> they took my money for a song i wrote in 2010, and haven't

---

1 https://hilltop-records.pissedconsumer.com/review.html

HELLO, SCAMMER

heard nothing from them since. i need answers NOW!
Loss: $400

Never did what they promised, and took my money
Tried to contact them got no response, its 5 yrs now.
They rush me saying my brother song was ready for production but after taking my money no action was taken. I am still heart broken

No production done
They contacted me after i submitted my song to copy rights office. They sent me a letter stating they were looking for country style songs for their AMERICA album. So i sent a demo cd of my country song i wrote. i was told its was great and made the finals and they were willing to produce it professionally and shop it for me. They said it would cost $324, so i paid the entire amount. I still have the contract with them to produce the song since july 2004. i paid $324 and it was never produced, never heard anything back from them since..i kept the my contract hoping for a class action suit..

I wrote song for Hilltop records called IN REMEMBRANCE
They contacted me, sent me a contract, And said I had to pass ' and I did. I'm on the Album called IN REMEBRANCE. My song is # 21 my name is Noah dr. bop the motorcity rocker, I paid close to $400.00 seems like for nothing I could have kept that money in my pocket, not theirs. All this happened around 2010. I've tried to contact them an no respond , and now this is 2018, and I need answers about my song. they wanted me to send more songs but I didn't because, I don't have money to waist #I NEED ANSWERS.

My first encounter with song sharks was as a young music student in college. One day a letter showed up in the mail that essentially said: We understand you're a songwriter. We want to hear your songs! You could be famous and rich!! I got more than one. Here is one of them.

HELLO, SCAMMER

SUNRISE RECORDS, INC.

Dear Songwriter/Lyricist;

We are pleased to have discovered through our different sources, such as music festivals, copyright and other recording/publishing companies, that you are a songwriter/lyricist, of which I am sure you are aware that songwriting is a multi-million dollar business. Last year songwriters made millions of $dollars$ from royalties received from their songwriting efforts.

Bear in mind . . . never in history has the demand for new songs been so great. Why? The reason is clear. The answer lies in the need for new material, and it is this constant need for new songs that has opened the door to opportunity and success for new songwriters. Recording companies need new songs for their recording artists. Without new songs they would cease to exist. Our quest is just this . . . we are looking for new song material for our recording artists. Just think how many new songs you hear on the radio from new recording artists. One day one of those songs could be yours! Just compare your songs with what is currently on the radio.

Many writers, perhaps like yourself, produce some really good songs/lyrics. They may be excellent and worthy of commercial recording. We offer a FREE EXAMINATION of all types of material; Pop, Rock, Ballads, Country-Western, Soul, Gospel-Christian, Rap, etc. And, all of our examinations are highly confidential. Your material can be copyrighted or without copyright, as your material is safe with us and will NOT be used without your consent.

ACT NOW, today . . . you may have real ability and by sending us your material YOU possibly could be the next songwriter collecting ROYALTIES from this multi-million dollar business.

LET US LOOK OVER YOUR WORK so that we may give you our honest opinion. As soon as we receive your material, it will be carefully examined and you will have our decision as quickly as possible, usually within two weeks. We ask that you submit no more than three (3) to five (5) of what you think are your best songs/lyrics and just follow these simple instructions for submission.

If submitting only lyrics or lead sheets:
1. Typed or printed clearly on separate sheets of paper.
2. Indication on each lyric/lead sheet the style of material, for example: ballad, rock & roll, pop, country-western, soul, christian, etc.
3. A self-addressed STAMPED envelope MUST be included for the return of your song material if not used.

If submitting a cassette tape:
1. Please submit ALL songs on one (1) cassette only.
2. Cassette MUST be accompanied by the written/printed works or a lead sheet (for clarity purposes).
3. Indication on each lyric/lead sheet the style of material, for example: ballad, rock & roll, pop, country-western, soul, christian, etc.
4. A self-addressed STAMPED envelope MUST be included for the return of your song material if not used.

It is with great pleasure that we are able to extend this invitation and opportunity in this, STILL very exciting music industry. Enclosed is a self-addressed envelope for your convenience in submitting your material. If, however, you have any questions regarding submission of material, our Songwriter Services Department will be glad to answer any questions you might have.

Sincerely,

Wade Wallace
Wade Wallace
Director of Music

7033 Sunset Boulevard, Suite 304, Hollywood, California 90028 — (213) 464-5200

HELLO, SCAMMER

Naïve, young me thought, "Wow! How did they know I'm a music writer? There must be something special about me." (At the time I did not know that they troll copyright registrations, all of which are public record. I had recently registered a piece with the Copyright Office). So I sent them a couple of my songs—songs that I would never pitch today—and some weeks later I received a letter back that my song had been accepted. Wow! Here's the acceptance letter:

HELLO, SCAMMER

SUNRISE RECORDS, INC.

November 1, 1991

Mr. Geoff Koch

RE: COMING TOGETHER

Dear Mr. Koch,

We are pleased to advise you that your above referenced song material is being considered for recording.

There are hundreds, and possibly even thousands of songs that could be, and someday will be, big sellers. New material, fresh ideas waiting to be discovered. We are right now trying to uncover some of these "hidden hits". We feel YOUR material contains the right ingredients for a commercial song.

If Sunrise Records decides to record your song commercially, we will ship records throughout the country to radio stations, disc-jockeys and record stores. And we will pay you a ROYALTY for each record sold.

Please understand that the recording industry is an extremely speculative business and should only be pursued by songwriters who can accept disappointment as well as success. Hundreds of records are released each week, only a few are "hits".

Please fill out the enclosed form and return to us at your earliest convenience.

Your material is being carefully examined and you should have our final decision within the next couple of weeks.

Sincerely,

SUNRISE RECORDS, INC.

Wade Wallace
Director of Music

WW/jp
Enclosure

7033 Sunset Boulevard, Suite 304, Hollywood, California 90028 — (213) 464-5200

HELLO, SCAMMER

Lost to time is the "enclosed form" referred to in the letter. The form was a "demo recording fee" plan—a contract—in which they would re-record the song to see if it was "good enough" to go on the aforementioned (but nonspecific) "record." This "record" was one they promised could earn me "ROYALTIES" just like songwriters who are making millions of dollars, so they said. Wow! But—the recording fee was hundreds of dollars (with easy installment payment plans!) which was a significant sum then for a broke college student. Still, I thought that if this is "how the industry works" maybe this would be my big break—I could whip out plastic and charge it (a.k.a. going into debt).

These were pre-internet days, so finding information about the legitimacy of this proposal was difficult. Thankfully, my college composition teacher had been in the music business since the 50's and was wise to these things. I showed him the letter and contract and he immediately was dubious. He made a few phone calls to various industry contacts and they all gave him the same story: not legit. A real music publisher/record company does not charge the songwriter to make a new recording of the song. If they're interested in the song and

HELLO, SCAMMER

deem a re-record necessary, it's on <u>their</u> dime, not the writer's. My teacher then got on the phone with the Sunrise Records and asked what exactly they want to charge me for. They could not provide a satisfactory answer. As he hung up, the situation became clear—my grand hopes had been hanging on a scammer. I was deflated. But at least I had dodged a scam and had not foolishly forked over a bunch of money I did not have.

Now I was onto them.

Fast-forward some years, some new copyright registrations, and a new round of song sharks came prowling.

In 2002, letters started arriving from "Hilltop Records". They were like the ones from previous song sharks years before, but with even more grandiose (but still vague) promises of tapping into the vast riches of the "multi-billion dollar music industry" and joining the ranks of stars like Dolly Parton and Willie Nelson. AND they want to hear my songs. Wow! Is it even possible for a letter to ooze more awesomeness? Yes, it is! Because the letter also said that if I write only lyrics, not music, not to worry, as <u>they</u> will write the music but <u>I</u> will own the song. Double-WOW!! Of course, this ought to be the first clue that something is amiss. Such a work would be considered a "co-write" or "co-authorship" and it makes no sense that co-writers would surrender their authorship share up front. (They probably had a cache of generic, wordless songs into which they could shoehorn any lyrics. This "record company" couldn't care less about the songs themselves.)

Unfortunately, this particular solicitation letter is also lost to time. However, what was in it can be easily ascertained from my response letter. Since I know knew their game I employed new tactic responding to them: I would compose the <u>stupidest</u>, <u>worst</u> songs imaginable and send it to them as serious submissions. So how much garbage can you throw at song sharks in order to get them to "bite" and accept it so they can charge me fees? Let's find out and mess with them…

HELLO, SCAMMER

7/20/02

Tom Hartman
Hilltop Records
1777 No. Vine Street, Ste. 411
Hollywood, CA 90028

Dear Tom Hartman,

I was so excited to receive your letter today! I've wanted for so long to join the likes of Dolly Parton and Willie Nelson in the multi-billion dollar music industry. With the enormous rate of growth in the music industry, radio stations constantly calling for new recordings, and new songs recorded and released every day (it's kind of hard to believe!), I realize that your letter to me could turn into my big break!

As you requested, I've enclosed five of my very best compositions. They're actually only lyrics and poetry at this point, because I'm not very good at music, but I know you can work some magic with them – if you think they're good enough. (I hope you will!) I've been working really hard on my songs for many years now and to have my song professionally packaged and shipped nationwide to stores and radio stations (plus royalties!!!) would be a dream come true.

I have lots more songs/poems in the works I could send you, but since you said "Don't delay" I'll just send you my finished stuff for right now. My mom and friends say my stuff is really good and suggested I start saving so I can record in a real studio someday. I've started doing just that and I can't wait!

I really hope you like what I send you – my songs all mean so much to me. I can't wait to hear back from you all! I'll be checking my mailbox every day!

Sincerely,

Geoff Koch

HELLO, SCAMMER

Since they said they can set my lyrics to song, I sent them a collection of awful haikus as my lyrical submission, suggesting each one could be turned into a song....

```
                  Good Haiku
                By Geoffrey Koch
    (To be turned into *Hit Songs* by Hilltop Records!)


              Rejection by you
          Hurts me in my spleen, oh yes
              Yes it does, yes... yes



           Heave ho, squeeze out songs
              Rejection's a laxative
              One more is done - plop.



              One two three four five
              I'm really quite prolific
              Five four three two one



              Billboard number one
          That's me on top!  Me on top!
              I'm better than you



              I will get to you
          Wait in line - other offer
          Better than yours - wait





              Copyright ©2002 Geoff Koch
```

HELLO, SCAMMER

And here's the envelope it was sent in

(Hilltop always got the leftover stamps).

So I waited and waited, and for some odd reason Hilltop Records executive producer, Tom Hartman, never got back to me. So weird. But that didn't stop Hilltop from coming back asking for more material.

In the summer of 2006, Hilltop sent me another letter (also lost to time) asking for Christmas songs for their upcoming album. Of course, I was happy to oblige with another submission of awfulness, accompanied by a wide-eyed cover letter, just for our Tom...

HELLO, SCAMMER

7/31/06

Tom Hartman
Hilltop Records
1777 No. Vine Street, Ste. 411
Hollywood, CA 90028

Dear Tom Hartman,

Hey! It's me! You know, I'm bummed that my prior submissions were not accepted. But you know, as my Aunt Naydgee always said, "There are times when you mind is being taken over by an… alien entity," so I knew I had to try again! So…

I heard that you guys are looking for Christmas songs for an upcoming Christmas album. Isn't that wild and KRAZY - writing Christmas songs in July? (That's "crazy" with a "K" for extra zaniness, just so you know.) It's tough to get into the holiday spirit when it's 100 degrees outside, if you know what I mean! LOL!!! So, to help me get into the mood, I turned the A/C way down as low as it would go and put on a cozy turtleneck sweater (red & green LOL!!!). Then I made up a batch of eggnog (ok, with a dash of Makers Mark - call me naughty. LOL!!!) Then I put a dab of Christmas cinnamon-fragranced Candle-Lite™ into the potpourri and let 'er rip. Then I was going to actually put up a little evergreen tree and don it with this neat antique angel tree topper, but nobody sells little evergreen trees this time of year, not even Wal-Mart! Isn't that KRAZY? But then I thought that maybe I could put up the artificial tree that was tucked way back in the corner of the attic. That would be awesome. But then I realized that it's way back in the corner, I mean WAY back in the corner. Like behind Aunt Naydgee's home-canned butterbeans, the broken rocker, and the Six-Million Dollar Man Board Game. Like I'm gonna move all of that stuff - I'm not crazy! LOL!!! (Notice the "crazy" with the "C" because I'm not the zany variety of crazy). Anyway, so are you getting the picture? The setting is about as perfect as you can get for Christmas in July. I was oozing with inspiration. I think I came up with one of the best Christmas/holiday songs that has been come up with in a while. Here's the jist…

Realistic Christmas - isn't that a cool concept for a Christmas song? I mean, in the midst of opening presents and eating cookies and stuff, "normal life" still goes on,

HELLO, SCAMMER

like your intestinal tract is still functioning, isn't it? So what better "angle" is there for a new Christmas song? None, I say! LOL!!! So let me introduce you to: *"Very Much Fart: An Ode to Yuletide Cheer."* It's one of my best songs, ever! (But I always send you my best songs, Tom). This song is bound to move people. (Notice that I wrote it using a Christmas kind of font. That really helps set the mood and get you into the spirit!)

Like usual, I'm not super good with music (I'm just good with words, or "lyrics" as they're called in the songwriting world. But you probably know that already being the President of Hilltop Records! Man, you probably never even say the word "words," not even by mistake!) So I know your super-talented producers can set my *LYRICS* to some of the best music ever written. I can't wait to hear how this sounds! It's gonna be AWESOME, in a holiday-ee kind of way. We're gonna move some units, baby! (That's how a gold-record-laden music record VP might say it).

I have lots more songs/poems in the works I could send you, but since you said "Christmas songs" for now I'll just send you my finished Christmas stuff for right now. My mom and friends say my stuff is really good. I've saved up a whole bunch of bookoo bucks and I can't wait to have my songs recorded somewhere!

I really hope you like what I send you - my songs all mean so much to me. I can't wait to hear back from you all! I'll be checking my mailbox every day!

Sincerely,

Geoff Koch

HELLO, SCAMMER

Very Much Fart:
An Ode to Yuletide Cheer

I inducted myself today
In a very special way
So that's why I'd like to say…
………………………….hey

The source of your protraction
Of girly satisfaction
Or intractable reaction
Is really quite insane

(bridge)
You know that's why we always say
You know that's why we always say

(chorus)
Yuletide Cheer is here
Always this time of year
Incredible family joy
Woo-hoo, woo-hoo

The incredible, edible egg
Is a singularity in space-time
Or a 3rd level Paladin
Whose yolk is creamy good

So when we gather 'round
The fire so toasty and bright
We MUST very much fart
And then give it a light

(bridge)

(solo) bagpipe or electric guitar

(chorus)
Yuletide Cheer is here
Always this time of year
Incredible family joy
Woo-hoo, woo-hoo

HELLO, SCAMMER

While the good folks at Hilltop were undoubtedly stupefied into non-response by my brilliant Christmas song, they did summon the gumption to solicit more songs from me. Which, of course, meant coming up with another awful song and ridiculous cover letter.

> BONUS!
>
> Since Tom Hartman unceremoniously rejected "Very Much Fart", I have taken it upon myself to actually produce and record this masterpiece for your listening pleasure. Let's prove Tom Hartman wrong and make sure this becomes a hit!

LISTEN
CD 2, TRACK 22

HELLO, SCAMMER

HILLTOP RECORDS
IN THE HEART OF HOLLYWOOD

1777 No. Vine Street, Ste. 411 • Hollywood, CA 90028 • (323) 469-3366

November 1, 2006

Geoff Koch

Dear Geoff Koch,

I was watching the news on television a few nights ago and heard a reporter say that 100 more Americans had died this past month far from home. In Iraq. The television camera focused on a yellow ribbon tied around a big Oak Tree in the front yard of one of the slain soldiers, and then I heard the voice of a relative saying how proud he was that the young American had served his country. Died for his country. I thought about that family and about a life cut so short. I thought about the many blessings we have and take for granted. And even when political beliefs differ, I know that all Americans support our brave servicemen and women and are grateful for their sacrifices.

It is with gratitude and pride that HILLTOP RECORDS announces the production of **PROUD TO BE AN AMERICAN**, a digitally recorded, CD album project. We are searching for the best, new, heartfelt, uniquely American songs for this remarkable production. We want songs that praise God, that pay homage to a fallen soldier, that celebrate small town America, that sing about the girl next door, or the truck driver, or the family you love – songs that are truly American in their perspective, their language and in their style.

Our great writers and musicians have played on stage and/or recorded with **Trisha Yearwood, Neil Diamond, Barry Manilow, Barbra Steisand, Celine Dion, Ray Charles, Tony Bennett, Linda Hopkins** and **Dolly Parton**. And this outstanding professional team will be writing, arranging and recording all the songs included in the **PROUD TO BE AN AMERICAN** CD project. In our search for great new American songs, we are inviting you to submit material for review. Songwriters chosen to participate in this project are by invitation only. **No unsolicited material will be accepted**.

In order to see a broad range of your work, please send us 2 or 3 poems, lyrics or songs - this increases your chances for acceptance. Send us songs about everyday life in America, or Gospel songs affirming your belief in God, or lyrics or poems praising the beauty of our countryside, life in our cities, the love of a dear one or the heroes in our midst.

If you write lyrics or poems but not music, and if a lyric or poem of yours is chosen for this CD album project, then our professional writers will put your words to music, and you will own the finished song.

A brilliant recording of a truly fine song can lift the spirit. It can heal a grieving heart. It can say thank you. It can bring unity, a feeling of joy and gratitude for the blessings that we share as Americans. If, like us, you are proud to be an American, let's say it by using our musical talents and give America its music. **PROUD TO BE AN AMERICAN** will be released on CD and sent to radio stations and stores across the country, and CD's will mailed to our servicemen and women over seas. If you want your music to be a part of this historic, timely CD project, send your material to HILLTOP RECORDS, **PROUD TO BE AN AMERICAN**, and send it right away.

All the best,

Tom Hartman, Executive Producer
HillTop Records, Inc.

SpclPTB/10-06

HELLO, SCAMMER

PROUD TO BE AN AMERICAN

HILLTOP RECORDS

HELLO, SCAMMER

1/24/07

Tom Hartman
Hilltop Records
1777 No. Vine Street, Ste. 411
Hollywood, CA 90028

Dear Tom Hartman,

Hey! It's me! Again. You know, I'm just so totally BUMMED that my prior submissions were not accepted. But you know, as my Aunt Naydgee always said, "If at first you don't succeed: bang your head on a step corner over and over again." So, if y'all don't start taking some of my songs, I'm going to have a HUGE knot on my forehead. LOL!!!   Ow.

Well, let me start off by saying that I was SO proud to get your last letter. **"Proud to be an American."** Wow. What a great concept for an album. I was so proud, in fact, that I saluted your letter as I read it. But you know what was really unbelievable about your letter? (You're gonna get shivers down your spine when you hear this!) Ok, check this out… You started off by saying:

> "*I was watching the news on television a few nights ago and heard a reporter say that 100 more Americans had died past month far from home. In Iraq…*"

You know what, Tom? I was watching that EXACT SAME TV show just a few nights ago, too!!! Isn't that just crazyweird??? (I made up that word myself: crazyweird). So you know, Tom – we've got this synergistic thing going, you and I do. I think we're like totally on the same wavelength on this album. I think that explains why the my last few submissions didn't make it on – you know, cuz the karma-bond wasn't jiving. But NOW… we're like, totally locked like something that's locked together in a karma-bonded-like locked-state.

SO… Tom, you're looking for the "best, new, heartfelt, uniquely American songs." I spent countless days pondering this mission for which you have commissioned me. And I finally came up with the perfect American song. Boy, do I have a treat for you!

(over, please)…

HELLO, SCAMMER

Introducing… the next HIT song on Hilltop Records:

America:
Free to Pee

Yes, what makes this great, vast land of ours so great are the so many, many places we can pee. Yes, there have got to be like a BILLION places where you can bleed the lizard in America. A TRILLION locales to shake the dew off the lily. It literally blows the mind (but not the bladder thankfully - LOL!!!). And to think those brave American soldiers DIED so that we can make yellow snow, I get humble lump in my throat. (And then I go pee).

This has to be one of the best patriotic songs ever written, and its genesis is all due to your letter, Tom. Thank heaven above for you and Hilltop Records, Tom.

Like usual, your professional writers can make the beautiful music to go along with this song, so I won't even bother with notes and stuff. Actually, "America: Free to Pee" is so pungent that it really doesn't even need music! (But it's still a song!) Crazyweird, isn't it? How about them apples, Tom?!

I really hope you like what I send you – my songs all mean so much to me. I can't wait to hear back from you! I'll be checking my mailbox every day!

Sincerely,

Geoff Koch

HELLO, SCAMMER

AMERICA: FREE TO PEE
By Geoffrey

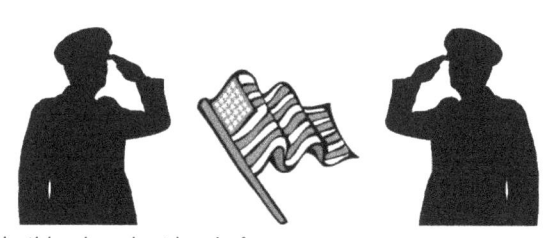

In this abundant land of ours
From sea to shining sea
Let's take some time and thank our troops
For so many places to pee

A toilet's nice, a urinal's fine
But there are other places, too
Like rivers, streams and subway trains
Where you might could also poo

> America – Free to pee!
> A place to go for you and me
> America – Free to pee!
> Let's hear it for #1 and take a leak with glee

U.S.A! U.S.A! U.S.A! U.S.A!

LISTEN
CD 2, TRACK 23

©Geoff Koch ← that means don't steal the song!!

304

HELLO, SCAMMER

Strangely, Hilltop never got back to me regarding my submission "America: Free to Pee." Perhaps they were still in awe of "Very Much Fart: An Ode to Yuletide Cheer." But they did get back to me soliciting songs for yet another Christmas album...

HELLO, SCAMMER

HILLTOP RECORDS
IN THE HEART OF HOLLYWOOD

1777 No. Vine Street, Ste. 411 • Hollywood, CA 90028 • (323) 469-3366

July 12, 2007

Geoff Koch

Dear Geoff Koch,

I'm writing with Magic in mind... Christmas Magic. We have just put together a team of musicians and arrangers including a CHORUS comprised of award-winning professionals. Some of our players have recorded tracks or performed with **Celine Dion, Natalie Cole, Trisha Yearwood, Harry Connick, Jr., George Strait, Dolly Parton, Tony Bennett,** and **Barry Manilow**. Our singers have been featured soloists with major singing groups and world-renowned chorales... two are GRAMMY nominees. One is a GRAMMY winner! These fabulous professionals will record HILLTOP's Christmas CD project. I'm writing to invite you to submit material for possible CD album inclusion.

With great excitement HILLTOP RECORDS announces **THE MAGIC OF CHRISTMAS,** a CD album edition for Christmas 2007. All songs reviewed for this professional project will be by invitation only. *No unsolicited material will be accepted.* We are looking for only the finest new Christmas songs, carols, lyrics and poems. My staff and I think your track record shows that you have the talent to write a magical Christmas song.

If at all possible, send 2 or 3 lyrics or songs. This will increase your chances for CD album inclusion. We are looking for popular as well as religious material, and we are currently reviewing songs, carols, lyrics and poems. If you write words but not music, and if one of your lyrics is chosen for the CD project, our professional writers will put your words to music, and **you will own the finished song.** All songwriters with a song included on **THE MAGIC OF CHRISTMAS** will be paid royalties for every CD sold.

This will be an exceptional, polished production. We have great, award-winning professional musicians. We have outstanding soloists and a chorus. We know we can produce "classic" recordings like "Silent Night" and "Rudolph." Now all we need is a magical, new Christmas song or carol from you, a talented songwriter.

Let's share the Magic... the Magic of beautiful Christmas music... share it with family and friends and with servicemen and women overseas. **THE MAGIC OF CHRISTMAS** will be sent to radio stations serving our Armed Forces, and if you have a dear one in the service, just give us the name and we will send that soldier a free CD for Christmas. No matter what our political beliefs, I'm sure that all Americans support the individuals who are willing to sacrifice their very lives for their Country. A Christmas CD with a song written by you might "bring them home" for just a moment and remind them that they are not forgotten at this blessed Holiday time. If you have written a song or poem that sings of family... of Santa... of Angels proclaiming the miraculous birth of the Child... that sings of **THE MAGIC OF CHRISTMAS,** send it to us at HILLTOP, and don't delay. Because of distribution plans and because we will put CD's in the hands of Americans serving far from home at Christmas, we must make song selections within the next few weeks. Send your Christmas songs or lyrics to my attention right away. We might make magic together... your song could be released on a Christmas CD recorded by some of the great musicians who have recorded songs for **Celine Dion, Trisha Yearwood, Natalie Cole** and **Tony Bennett.**

All the best,

Tom Hartman, Executive Producer

SPCLXM2007

HELLO, SCAMMER

HELLO, SCAMMER

11/7/07

Tom Hartman
Hilltop Records
1777 No. Vine Street, Ste. 411
Hollywood, CA 90028

Re: *The MAGIC of Christmas*

Dear Tom Hartman,

Hey! It's me! I gotta tell ya Tom, ever since I got your letter last July asking for songs for your upcoming CD *"The Magic of Christmas!"* (*Christmas fonts help me get in the mood! LOL!!!*) I've been working, working, working! Man have I been working. I mean, how often do you get a chance to have your very own SONG recorded on a CD by unbelievable award-winning professionals? And by invitation only? That's KRAY-ZEE good fortune! Kind of like when you go through the drive-thru at McDonald's and they ask you: "Would you like to BIGGIE size that?" And you say, "Nah." But they BIGGIE size it anyway without charging extra! (probably by mistake, but like I'm gonna say something! Yeah, right! LOL!!!) And then they accidentally give you an extra McDonald's Monopoly game piece, to boot. Woah. That's extra KRAY-ZEE good fortune!!! Like my Aunt Naydgee always said: "Getting good fortune is like eating a fortune cookie - eventually it pops out the other end!"

You know, Tom, I'm bummed that my prior submissions were not accepted. But you know, as my Aunt Naydgee always said, "If at first you fail, switch brands and do the exact same thing over again!" so I knew I had to try again! So…

It being November and all and my mind on turkey and all, I gotta admit that it can be a challenge to think beyond to Christmas - you know, with my mind on Butterball and stuffing and Pilgrims and stuffing and Macy's parade and stuff, who wants to think about opening presents??? You know I'm a one-thing-at-a-time kind of guy, Tom! LOL!!! But since we're talking about unbelievable professionals who have done things and stuff with **Celine Dion**, **Natalie**

308

HELLO, SCAMMER

Cole and Barry Manilow (love that Copacabana!!!) with a CHORUS performing my very own song, how can I say no to you, Tom? So let me tell you how I've been rolling up the sleeves and hammering out hits for you, Tom...

Since July I've written about 50 hit songs for you and Hilltop Records - half of them (that's 25) will be #1 hits. And of those 25, 10 of them will remain #1 on Billboard for 10 weeks or more. That could be a whole lotta gold records for both you and me, Tom!!!! But then I realized something, Tom - why submit 50 hit songs when I've already written the one, perfect song? It's like trying to reinvent the wheel, Tom. I mean, can you make the wheel any more rounder than it is now? No, silly! Or what about chicken on a stick? Can you improve on that? Duh. NO. (Like what are you gonna do - put chicken on an empty toilet paper roll?) Likewise with me and my one, perfect Christmas song...

Very Much Fart: An Ode to Yuletide Cheer

Doesn't the title just warm the soul and make you want to quaff eggnog? I know, it has that effect on everybody!

So, all I did with the song, Tom, (since I submitted it to you once before - I'm not sure why it wasn't accepted) is to re-arrange it for CHOIR. I get goose pimples just thinking about it. (You just got 'em, too, admit it!!!) So for *"The Magic of Christmas!"* I give you "Very Much Fart: An Ode to Yuletide Cheer." (This song will probably be good for both the opening AND closing track on the CD).

Like usual, I'm not super good with music (I'm just good with words, or "lyrics" as they're called in the songwriting world. But you probably know that already being the President of Hilltop Records! Man, you probably never even say the word "words," not even by mistake!) So I know your super-talented producers who have recorded tracks with **Celine Dion, Natalie Cole and Barry Manilow** (love that Copacabana!!!) can set my *LYRICS* to some of the best music ever written. I can't wait to hear how this

HELLO, SCAMMER

sounds! It's gonna be AWESOME, in a holiday-ee kind of way. We're gonna move some units, baby! (That's how a gold-record-laden music record VP might say it).

Now Tom, I know we've already discussed the perfection thing and all with this song, but you did ask for at least 2 songs from me, so I'll give you one more song of mine written specially for your CHOIR called: "Christmas - Curiously Cozy." This song doesn't have any instruments on it, just the CHOIR singers singing (also known as "a cappella," but as executive producer, you knew that, Tom didn't you???!!!) The lyrics consist of soothing oo's and mm's. Once your unbelievable super-talented producers who have recorded tracks with **Celine Dion, Natalie Cole and Barry Manilow** (love that Copacabana!!!) set these lyrics to music, this one will chart at #2 Billboard, just behind Very Much Fart. I can't wait to hear it!!!!

I can't wait to hear back from you, Tom! You and me, Tom - we're headed for the top! I'll be checking my mailbox every day!

Delightfully yours,

Geoff Koch

HELLO, SCAMMER

Christmas – Curiously Cozy

Words by Geoff Koch
(Music to be written by *professional writer* Tom Hartman)!!!!

(choir - a cappella
that means NO INSTRUMENTS!!!)

Words by Geoff Koch
(Music to be written by professional writer
Tom Hartman)!!!!

(choir - a cappella
that means NO INSTRUMENTS!!!)

(verse 1)
Mmmmm mmmmm mmmmm mmmm
Mmm   mm mm Mmmm   mmmm
Mmmmm mmmmm mmmmm mmmm
M Mmm Mm Mmmmmmmmmmmm...

(verse 2)
Mmmmm mmmmm mmmmm mmmm
Mmm   mm mm Mmmm   mmmm
Mmmmm mmmmm mmmmm mmmm
M Mmm Mm Mmmmmmmmmmmm...

(Chorus)
Ooooo ooooo oo oooooo
Ooooo ooooo oo ooo oo
O Oo Oo Ooooooooo

(verse 3)
Mmmmm mmmmm mmmmm mmmm
Mmm   mm mm Mmmmmm   mmmm
Mmmmm mmmmm mmmmm mmmm
Mmm mmm mmmmmm
M Mmm Mm Mmmmmmmmmmmm...

HELLO, SCAMMER

(bridge)
Ahhh ahhh ahhhhhhhhh
Ah ah ahahahhhhhhh

(Chorus)
Ooooo ooooo oo oooooo
Ooooo ooooo oo ooo oo
O Oo Oo Oooooooo...

(Upon the completion of the song, allow for a long pause such that the listener may reflect upon what he/she just heard and contemplate the many reasons Christmas is Curiously Cozy.)

HELLO, SCAMMER

HELLO, SCAMMER

For some weird reason after, this last resubmission of "*Very Much Fart: An Ode to Yuletide Cheer*" and "*Christmas – Curiously Cozy*" I never heard back from Hilltop Records ever again. That made me so very sad. So, so sad.

But the story does not quite end there yet.

* * *

In the fall of 2019 I paid a visit to **1777 No. Vine Street** in Hollywood, Hilltop Record's business address, the physical location where my numerous garbage submissions were delivered. Security guards working inside said there was no company in the building by that name. A search of businesses on the California Secretary of State's website showed that Hilltop Records had been defunct since 2017 – out of business, corporation dissolved. No more.

Hilltop Records was gone.

It was a rather satisfying conclusion to a scam that had been running for decades. I'd like to think I played a small part in their demise. That evening I went home happy.

Hello, scammer.

Goodbye.

HELLO, SCAMMER

Enjoying the last laugh at the former home

of Hilltop Records

HELLO, SCAMMER

ABOUT THE AUTHOR

Geoff is a composer and producer of original music for nationally and internationally broadcast television shows, films, commercials, jingles, planetarium shows, station image promos, corporate/industrial works, songs and other media. This Iowa native's music has been heard in everything from *Saturday Night Live* to the National Geographic Channel to feature films to planetariums around the world for over two decades. Some of his earliest musical explorations included joke songs and novelty jingles for nonexistent products – fertile ground for eventually messing with scammers in unorthodox ways.

He earned his Bachelor of Music between Oberlin Conservatory and Belmont University's commercial music program, was featured in Keyboard Magazine in 1996 and had his first choral piece accepted for publication when he was just twenty. Upon graduating college, he was tapped to serve as pianist for Grand Ole Opry star *Lorrie Morgan*'s "Christmas In London" national

HELLO, SCAMMER

tour. He has also served as pianist/keyboardist for *The Glenn Miller Orchestra, Restless Heart*, and most recently, 2009 Rock and Roll Hall of Fame inductees, *Little Anthony and The Imperials*. He is the recipient of the distinguished 2015 Curtain Call Award, a two-time Hollywood Music in Media Awards nominee, as well as numerous other broadcast and industry awards such as the ADDY Awards. He serves as the current president of the *Nashville Composers Association*, www.nashvillecomposers.org and has yet found time to mess with telemarketers and scammers. There is *always* time to mess with scammers.